ALSO BY RICHARD DAVIS, Ph.D.

The Intangibles of Leadership: The 10 Qualities of
Superior Executive Performance

GOOD JUDGMENT

GOOD JUDGMENT

**Making Better Business Decisions
with the Science of Human Personality**

RICHARD DAVIS, PH.D.

HARPER
BUSINESS

An Imprint of HarperCollins*Publishers*

HarperCollins books may be purchased for educational, business, or sales promotional use. For information, please email the Special Markets Department at SPsales@harpercollins.com.

FIRST EDITION

Designed by Michele Cameron

Library of Congress Cataloging-in-Publication Data has been applied for.

ISBN 978-0-06-329367-0

24 25 26 27 28 LBC 5 4 3 2 1

To Eva, Brandon, Aaron, and Lauren,
who inspire me in immeasurable ways

CONTENTS

READER'S NOTE

THROUGHOUT THIS BOOK, I recount stories from my clients—the good, bad, and ugly. These are real stories about real people. In some cases, I've changed names and other identifying details for confidentiality. In others, I've been able to speak more openly. Regardless, I hope these stories help to convey my underlying point about the importance of perceptivity. We all face difficult choices concerning people as we go about our lives. If we get these choices right, we'll ultimately be happier and more successful.

INTRODUCTION

DURING THE LATE 1970S and early '80s, when I was a boy, my parents and I attended hockey games, concerts, and other events together, taking long subway rides around my hometown of Toronto, Canada. To pass the time in transit, Mom and I played what we called "the game." When someone with an intriguing appearance sat down across from us, Mom would elbow me and whisper, "What do you think?" That was my cue to invent an elaborate narrative about this stranger, one that was plausible enough, but wholly theoretical.

Let's say it was a Sunday afternoon, and a businessman in his late twenties wearing a finely tailored, pinstriped suit got on carrying a heavy bag of groceries. This man was dark-haired, slender, and wore a wedding ring. He was freshly shaven. He carried a newish-looking leather briefcase in addition to the groceries. He seemed tired and a bit jittery.

Getting the elbow from my mom, I'd lean over and mutter, "Okay, the guy's name is Mike, his last name is . . . Simpson. Mike works at a bank, and his wife, whose name is Cheryl and who also works at the bank, is eight months' pregnant. Even though it's Sunday, Mike's overbearing boss made him come in to help him finish up a big project. His boss was old-school, so he expected Mike to dress up."

Taking another furtive glance at "Mike," Mom would nod and encourage me to continue.

"So here's what happened," I might have said. "Mike and his boss just began their work when Cheryl called. She was feeling sick and had a craving for pickles and ice cream. She wondered if Mike would be a dear and bring her some as well as a few other groceries they needed. Mike is a nice guy and deeply in love with his wife—he just can't say no to her. So even though he knew he'd get in trouble with his boss, he excused himself and went to go pick up the pickles and ice cream."

These stories went on and on like this. When "Mike" got off at his stop and someone else with an interesting vibe sat down, we'd start a new story and spool that one out as far as we could. It was great fun, and the subway rides flew by.

For many years, I didn't think too much of these stories. Our game was just that—a game. By the time I reached my twenties, though, I realized that this distraction had taught me to become keenly observant of the world around me, and perhaps more importantly, to develop a rich vocabulary for describing people. Wherever I went, I tended to notice others and their behavior, down to the smallest details—how they spoke, how they carried themselves, how they dressed, how others responded to them.

I never really stopped playing "the game." Today it's not much of a stretch to say that I make a living doing it. I'm an organizational psychologist specializing in the assessment of personality. Personality traits determine our behaviors, encompassing as they do our motivations, values, social inclinations, reactions to crisis or complexity, and patterns of thinking, among other things. If you want to make sound decisions about people, you'll need to be able to predict how they will likely behave. And the best way of doing that is to understand their personalities.

Put another, more unusual way, with the help of well-established science and artful experience, I judge people for a living. Some of the world's biggest, most recognizable companies hire me to quickly size up leadership candidates and potential partners to inform their decision-making. I also coach high-profile CEOs and their key executives, helping them raise their games and navigate job complexities. My value to these leaders hinges on my ability to generate penetrating insights into who they are, what makes them tick, and how they come across to others. Applying what we might call *perceptivity*—the ability to discern the character of others and reliably predict their behavior on the basis of said character—I develop an accurate reading of my clients' inherent traits and advise these leaders accordingly.

Such science-based assessments have important practical applications. Many of the companies I work with face critically important business decisions about people, such as which candidate they should hire as their new CEO, whether they should acquire another company and its leadership team, or how to handle difficult personnel matters. In making such decisions, my clients typically consider traditional criteria like an individual's experience and track record, educational background, interpersonal impact, strategic thinking ability, professional reputation, and so on. Increasingly, companies also consider factors like individuals' "emotional intelligence" (more on this concept—and its shortcomings—later) and their personal values. Before these companies proceed, however, they ask me to come in and explore the *character* of the people they're going to hire or place a bet on, because character is what truly sets successful candidates apart from the rest. Do these individuals have the specific temperament and behavioral inclinations they'll need to succeed? If not, it's essential to know now. If so, what do companies need to do early on to integrate these new hires most smoothly into their organization?

My conclusions often have profound impacts, both personal and commercial. A person's career might be made or ended. A company or team might thrive or fail, get acquired or be ignored. In my assessment process, I administer formal psychological tests to give me a rough sense of an individual's personality, but the real magic lies in a very specific, three-hour interview I have crafted over the course of my career. During this semi-structured session, I show curiosity about my interviewee's personal journey and ask them to take me chronologically through their story. Our individuality is in many ways a function of our lived experiences, so I ask interviewees to describe pivotal experiences in their lives. This interview is semi-structured because while it follows a deliberate methodology, I intend it to feel natural and be flexible. It's not a formal encounter like a job interview, but rather the sort of informal, reflective talk you might expect to have over a beer or glass of wine.

During this assessment, I ask the person about their parents, their childhood, what college was like for them, and so on. I inquire about decisions they made, the friends they had, and the values they learned as kids. I ask them to reflect on how their life experiences influenced who they are today. Rather than rely on a preset list of questions and attempt to draw out specific answers, I pose just the right questions to reveal true character. In processing their responses, I'm focused squarely on their personalities—how diligent they are, how outgoing, how prone to strategic thinking, and much more—in order to discern whether these individuals possess the specific traits that my clients require of them, and further, whether they tend to express those traits in specific ways suitable to my clients' goals.

A company's board might need its next CEO to be decisive, focused, and a strong communicator. Investors backing a start-up might want its leader to be not only a visionary but also capable of working well with others and accepting constructive feedback, and so on. Will the individuals under consideration fit these criteria? And do they possess any qualities that, given the specific role they'll have to play, might prove destructive? I assess individuals for relevant traits they might have and give my clients a clear answer: yes, or no.

I've assessed thousands of individuals over the past two decades for companies in industries like professional sports, technology, fashion, and global banking, and on every continent except Antarctica (although I have visited there as a tourist, and it is stunning!). When clients ignore my recommendations—for instance, hiring someone whose personality I consider ill-suited to the role for which they're being considered—they almost always find that the traits I warned them about come back to haunt them.

One client of mine, a private equity firm, was about to invest in a fast-growing company that had already bought up a number of small medical practices across the United States, bundled them together, and was now running them as one organization. In general, the value of medical practices that are bundled together significantly exceeds the value of these practices when run as independent businesses. If this company could accelerate its acquisition and integration of practices, the private equity firm stood to make tens of millions or more on the deal. Similar health care roll-up strategies have created billions of dollars in value.

When the private equity firm came to me, they had already run their detailed financial analysis, had assessed the strategic plan, and had run a legal review. Everything looked good, and they were ready to do the deal. Still, as part of their due diligence, they wanted to confirm one more thing—that the leaders of this consolidating company had what it took to execute the proposed strategy and scale the business according to their expectations.

Upon interviewing the key players for several hours and applying the framework you'll learn about in this book, I spotted a big problem. The CEO of the consolidating company—I'll call him Jay—was smart and well organized, but he had personality traits that would impede him from growing this company. Skeptical by nature, he held strong points of view and didn't change his mind easily. Rather than embrace change and pursue progress, he gravitated toward tradition and to what had worked in the past. Jay was also a prickly character—reserved, restrained, unempathetic. Although he cared about others, he didn't show it. Finally, it became obvious that Jay wasn't motivated very much by commercial interests (yes, private equity firms want their CEOs to be motivated by money) or even by a passion for his work. What he cared about was maintaining a sense of independence, being in control of his destiny. He just wanted to do his own thing.

Based on my assessment, I concluded that Jay wouldn't be able to grow his company much more than he already had. His success so far at convincing medical doctors to sell their practices to his company looked good on paper, but he had relied on long-standing personal relationships and hadn't adhered to a sound acquisition strategy. He didn't have the people skills or the flexibility to sell his strategy to doctors across the country, nor would he be able to adapt well to the new demands of running a much-larger organization. On a personal level, he would be a terrible partner for my private equity client. Because he needed autonomy and didn't really like feedback, he would feel stifled by support from my client and other members of the company's board of directors, regardless of their positive intention. Viewing the board's advice as impinging on his independence, he most likely would reject it outright.

I counseled the private equity firm to walk away from the deal. My clients bristled at this advice. They had already sunk hundreds of thousands of dollars into performing due diligence and the business looked strong on paper. In the end, though, they listened to me. Good thing: other investors put money into this venture, and a few years later it flamed out completely because Jay and his team couldn't grow the business, as I had predicted based on my assessment of him. "Thank God we didn't do this deal," my client later said to me. "We would have lost our shirts."

The ability to read others' personalities quickly and accurately, overcoming biases and prejudices that might skew our perception, is critical when making decisions and managing relationships both professional and personal. I would argue it's among the most fundamental aspects of judgment, and perhaps one of the most fundamental human skills in general. Possessing certain other skills related to judgment, such as the ability to reason critically, take a long-term view, manage risk, and think ethically, helps us to arrive at good decisions. But the most difficult and consequential decisions we face—whom to marry, what job to take, which business partner to take on, what tactic to adopt in a big negotiation—almost always hinge on judgments we must make about the people involved. Good judgment is, in essence, good *people* judgment. In this regard, the prehistoric human skill of determining whether someone is a friend or a foe has evolved over time to become a powerful tool that separates those who thrive from those who don't.

You might be thinking at this point about another widely discussed ability associated with judgment: emotional intelligence (EQ). Over the past two decades, popularizers of EQ have presented it as a panacea for anything that negatively impacts personal and leadership behavior. Some of you reading this undoubtedly believe that we all need EQ to make better decisions and perform better. Let me state here, as a licensed psychologist whose peers have sometimes been similarly duped, that what you have heard about

EQ

emotional intelligence is largely overblown and minimally effective. EQ sounds good, it feels right, we can wish that it were a real concept in its popularized form, but it just isn't.

A basic tenet of EQ is the value of emotions in human behavior. I wholeheartedly agree: emotions are important, and the ability to read and respond to others' emotions is the essence of empathy. However, because emotions are transitory, they don't tell us very much about how a person will behave long-term. Personality traits, by contrast, are stable and consistent. If we wish to cultivate good judgment, gaining insight into someone's emotional state is much less powerful than understanding their character traits (and our own, too).

Imagine that you had a kind of secret X-ray vision when it came to people—an uncanny ability to see past what others might want you to know about them and instead see who they actually *are*. Employees you hire would thrive because they'd have the right capabilities and temperament for the job. Your relationships with business partners, colleagues, customers, vendors, bosses, and others would last longer and be more fulfilling because you'd be better able to manage and deepen those connections. You'd like your job more, because you would surround yourself with people who would contribute to your success rather than get in the way. Almost every relationship at work and indeed in your life would function better if you exercised good judgment based on your insights into others' personalities. You would choose the right people and understand better how to nurture relationships over time, interpreting others' actions and responding to them in more productive ways.

You might think good judgment isn't something you can obtain—that you're either born with it or else unable to acquire it with age, maturity, and experience. It's true that some highly successful people do seem to have a gut instinct for assessing people, and that older people possess better judgment thanks to their life experiences and the wisdom they've accumulated (grandparents, for example, seem to just *know* about people). But there's another route to becoming a good judge of personality, one that has made a huge difference in my own career: applying powerful insights and techniques from the science of human personality.

Early scholars within the field of psychology tended to focus on our collective experience rather than on what makes us unique as individuals—our personalities. They studied the "human condition," or the nature of human behavior and why we behave the way we do as a species. This type of research culminated most famously in Sigmund Freud's early but brilliant work on the different levels of consciousness and the underlying mechanisms that drive human behavior. Such research also gave rise to social psychology, which studies our behavior in social contexts, our natural biases, and the environment's impact on our behavior. Over time, however, psychologists became more interested in understanding individual differences, the characteristics that differentiate you from me. This study of individual differences is what we now call personality psychology.

Two key insights emerged from this research. First, human beings are far more knowable to ourselves and others than we think. Second, we can distill personality down to just a handful of *dimensions* of inherent characteristics, otherwise known as traits. Scientists differ in exactly what these dimensions are, but the most commonly accepted scientific model of personality—often called the Big Five—corresponds to the acronym OCEAN: Openness, Conscientiousness, Extroversion, Agreeableness, and Neuroticism. As the science shows, we can describe our personality as a function of all five dimensions. We tend to be higher or lower in certain dimensions than in others, and we also tend to manifest specific traits differently in our behavior.

The practical implications of this research are enormous. Think about all the words you could use to describe someone. There are so many thousands of options that the task quickly becomes unwieldy. Isn't it reassuring to know that we can boil down this entire vocabulary to just five dimensions? Instead of driving ourselves crazy trying to analyze hundreds of personality traits when making important decisions about people, we can use a manageable personality framework (or one derived from it) to analyze character in the real world. Linking behaviors to the five dimensions, we can determine *patterns* in individual behaviors and on that basis qualitatively characterize people according to their traits. Adjusting for our own biases, we can wind up with an assessment of people that, although hardly exhaustive, is stunningly accurate and useful for practical purposes.

Personality frameworks are a uniquely powerful way of seeing the world. When trying to decide whom to hire, marry, become friends with, do business with, and so on, or when trying to better navigate relationships with others, you can quickly assess individuals and make better judgment calls. You can evaluate broad categories of traits along with the nuanced ways in which they are expressed simply by observing and interpreting behavior. It turns out that other people's deepest, most enduring tendencies—the traits that make them special and that determine whether they'll make good partners for you in work and in life—are right there for you to see, readily perceptible in how people move in the world. You just need to know how to look. This book teaches you, presenting a powerful, proven method you can use right now to enhance your life by judging the character of others more effectively.

Over the past two decades, I've greatly updated the observational skills I developed as a child, grafting on to them a version of the framework described above as well as other science-based tools and techniques for sizing people up quickly and accurately. Drawing on decades of research, including some of the most empirically validated findings in all of psychology, I've formed these into a concise, practical approach that allows you to discern whom someone you meet *really* is in a surprisingly short time. Mastering this approach requires practice, but its basic contours are so easy to learn that anyone can use it right away to improve their perceptivity, in any social context—and without a PhD in psychology. When you start using it, you're able to make better choices about people and steer relationships in desirable directions. Perhaps more importantly, you're able to understand *yourself* better and operate more effectively at work and in your personal life. And, as an added benefit, you become more alert to personality in *any* encounters you might have with others. As your general perceptivity increases, you can make good initial judgments about others you meet casually in your life, even if you haven't thought about forming relationships with them beforehand. You have an extra edge that helps you to interpret their behavior and inform how you engage with them in turn.

I've organized this book to give you a concise, useful introduction to the art and science of good judgment. In Chapter 1, I explain more thoroughly than I have done in this introduction why an ability to understand others' personality plays such an important role in our ability to interact effectively with others, and, in particular, why it's far more important than emotional intelligence. Chapter 2 presents a powerful framework of personality you can use, and explains its underlying science.

Next, I convey how you might adapt this basic method for practical purposes. In Chapter 3, I explain how to conduct conversations so that they yield maximum insight into others. Chapter 4 discusses how to select potential partners. Chapter 5 explains how to set relationships up for more success by understanding others' personalities. Chapter 6 explores how you can use my method to help yourself and others perform better and advance more quickly. Chapter 7 rounds out the book by showing you how to use my method to become more persuasive and influence others in all kinds of everyday situations.

I've written this book not only to share with you ways to improve your judgment, but because I am concerned that we are at grave risk of losing this elemental human capability. Since the introduction of GPS technology, younger people and even many of us adults have lost our ability to find our way in unknown surroundings. Something similar is happening with perceptivity—we're outsourcing this cognitive capability to our screens and are thus losing our insight into other people. If you're reading this in a public place right now, look around you. Chances are, most people aren't focusing on you or anyone else around them, but on their phones. It's pretty disturbing when you think about it. Many years ago, I did my doctoral research on overuse of and addiction to the Internet. Unfortunately, my research was way too prescient. We have succumbed to the digital world in a way that I feared, but with costs to humanity beyond what I predicted. Perceptivity is a cognitive muscle that makes us uniquely human, and by burying our heads in our screens, we allow any observational and interpretive skills we might have to atrophy.

Good Judgment can help. No matter how adept you are at sizing people up, the framework and tactics in this book will enable you to up your game. But I also intend this book as a rallying cry, inspiring you to take stock of others and their uniqueness once again. Put your devices down and play a version of the game I played on the subway with my mother so many years ago. Rediscover your child-

like curiosity about others and their inherently distinctive qualities. Further, let's appreciate and celebrate one another's unique
traits, and let's account for them in how we interact socially. If you
do, you'll not only enjoy more success in your career and personal
relationships—you'll also discover a more satisfying and human
way to live.

GOOD JUDGMENT

Chapter 1

PERSONALITY > EQ

FRANK, A BRILLIANT SOFTWARE entrepreneur, had a critical decision to make, one that hinged on his ability to assess others. Over the past several years, his firm had grown its core business to hundreds of millions of dollars in revenue. The firm was poised for even more impressive growth thanks to forthcoming product launches in new markets. But this rapid growth confronted Frank with a quandary: although he had poured so much of his focus into developing and managing the company's core product, he now needed to devote himself to overseeing the company's broader business portfolio. Another leader would have to step in to operate the core business, becoming president of the division and managing a team of hundreds while reporting to Frank.

After an extensive search, Frank wound up with three strong candidates for the job. One was a brilliant strategist currently working at a major Silicon Valley tech company. Frank knew him and had been his mentor for years. Another was a talented young executive who had worked at the company for a year and had already shown himself to be highly ambitious, loyal, and a big thinker. The third was another industry veteran who had distinguished himself in previous positions as an extremely hard worker and an exceptional decision-maker.

Frank had a lot of practice sizing people up over the course of building the company—it was a regular part of doing business. But never had the stakes been quite so high. If his core business faltered, he would have to drop everything else he was working on and reassume oversight. The company's other growth prospects would suffer, translating into tens of millions of dollars in lost revenues.

Our ability to judge people—including ourselves—looms large throughout our lives. It determines how adept we are at choosing others to partner with as bosses, employees, spouses, and friends. It also determines how well we manage relationships in our lives and how well we handle conflict when it arises. It even determines how effectively we steer our own path in life—our ability to pick a direction for ourselves and take meaningful steps along that path.

But what constitutes good judgment? Until a few decades ago, most people equated decision-making prowess with intelligence, assuming that people who make the right calls and judge others shrewdly are, above all, smart. That is, they are able to analyze data, understand complexity, and determine the right course of action almost intrinsically. They are also wise, possessing a perspective that is informed by their past experiences (a subject covered in my previous book, *The Intangibles of Leadership*). Today, people tend to point to something else: the ability to read, understand, and respond to emotions—what is popularly known as emotional intelligence, or EQ—claiming that it is what sets the successful apart. Some individuals just seem to "get" others' emotions and be in touch with their own. They're more empathetic, more aware of their own feelings, more sensitive toward others, and easier to get along with. As a result, the thinking goes, they tend to make better decisions than those who are weak in these areas, and they tend to communicate their decisions in ways that inspire and engage others around them.[1]

Consultants, journalists, and business leaders often present emotional intelligence as somehow more critical to success in business and in life than conventional intelligence.[2] In 2022, incoming New York City mayor Eric Adams proclaimed that emotional intelligence would be the "No. 1 criteria" he would use to pick top people for his administration, a trait more important, in his view, than raw intelligence or academic pedigree. "Don't tell me about your Ivy League degrees," he said. "I don't want to hear about your academic intelligence. I want to know about your emotional intelligence."[3]

But is emotional intelligence *really* the superpower we all need to make better decisions, manage relationships better, negotiate better, and generally reach our life and career goals? The answer is no. Emotional intelligence as popularly conceived is, to be blunt, bullshit. The popular definition of EQ is a mishmash of research-based EQ, aspects of personality, and common components of positive social behavior (for instance, being a nice person, showing empathy, and so on). EQ is appealing because it should mean that people who have more sensitive dispositions could be better leaders. We intuitively resonate with the idea that old, stodgy directive management styles don't work, and we presume that we need a new, more emotional kind of leadership. We have to be nicer, gentler, and more sensitive now. Nice people apparently don't finish last, don't ya know—it turns out they're more likely to finish first.

But are they really? Unfortunately, little, if any, evidence supports the idea that EQ actually predicts leadership success separate and apart from personality and general intelligence. The truth of the matter is that EQ has little actual effect on long-term success. New York City is a case in point. Despite Eric Adams's move to hire people based on their EQ, the city hasn't yet seen a renaissance in public management. On the contrary, residents have dealt with a rise in crime, worsening challenges with affordable housing, an immigration crisis, and a host of other socioeconomic issues.[4] Of course, these are all highly complex matters, involving state and federal policy, and Adams himself has demonstrated strong leadership impact at times. The point is that EQ is not some sort of leadership panacea and should not be the basis of a hiring strategy.

Another, more profound approach to judgment *does* have science behind it: the ability to understand and assess human personality, what I call perceptivity. EQ is about cueing into emotional states, which are largely fleeting. As research has shown, the chemical signature of emotions triggered by external stimuli lasts only about ninety seconds, although our own thought processes can prolong this response.[5] By contrast, our core temperaments—how creative, trustworthy, industrious, or sociable we are—remain constant, evolving at a slow pace, with changes only becoming apparent over a period of decades. I once read a journalist who likened personality traits to "tectonic plates shifting rather than an earthquake."[6] It's true: personality is stable. It doesn't change much, and in many ways it defines exactly who we are and how we differ from others. Personality is a deeply researched construct, one of the hallmarks of the science of psychology. We know a lot about personality, and it's as real as it gets. Perceptivity is about cueing into these core, stable traits and extrapolating how they affect people's ability to do something that needs to get done.

EQ can help us to recognize, say, anger in a manager or in a customer service representative, and adjust our style in the moment to navigate for that emotion. However, we're dealing with a moment in time, a transactional awareness of and a reaction to what we might assume is a stand-alone event. How much more powerful might it be to determine if someone is an *angry person*—that is, anger as a trait—and adjust our general approach to dealing with this person accordingly? Put another way, EQ helps us modestly understand how a person is experiencing a given situation, while perceptivity helps us robustly understand who a person *is*. If we can understand people and how they tick, and if we can learn to discern deeper personality traits by analyzing behavior, we enjoy a decisive edge when making decisions in business and in life. We can anticipate how people are likely to behave, and shape our decision-making accordingly. Perceptivity, not EQ, is truly the essence of good judgment.

EMOTIONAL INTELLIGENCE: HOW INTELLIGENT IS IT REALLY?

TO UNDERSTAND HOW UNSCIENTIFIC, unhelpful, and ultimately meaningless popular conceptions of EQ really are, it helps to consider the history of the term. Although scattered references to emotional intelligence appeared in scientific literature during the 1970s and '80s, the concept first received serious attention from scholars in a 1990 article by psychologists Peter Salovey and John D. Mayer.[7] As they pointed out, scholars had been studying cognition for decades and had discerned different types of intelligence. Most notably, the American psychologist Howard Gardner, in his famous theory of multiple intelligences introduced during the early 1980s, had argued that different modalities of intelligence exist and that people can show a range of abilities in each.[8] Gardner originally suggested seven types of intelligences: musical, spatial, verbal, mathematical, physical, social, and introspective. He later added naturalistic (understanding and being adept in nature) and existential (spiritual intelligence).

Naturally, Gardner's theory appealed to the public. Musical children may not score high on a traditional IQ test, but they could still be regarded as brilliant in their talents. A person with linguistic intelligence who just didn't get math should be deemed smart nonetheless. When introduced, Gardner's multiple intelligences gained popular support and sparked all kinds of publicity and research investigation by other scholars. Educational systems latched on to the theory and adjusted system-wide curricula to suit it (you've probably heard of "learning styles"—this is the conceptual basis for them).

In the decades that followed, however, researchers rigorously tested the theory and found that the multiple intelligences Gardner proposed were not at all valid.[9] These intelligences all correlate with our traditional definition of general intelligence, and nearly all psychologists now debunk the concept of learning styles (despite its appeal) as pseudoscience.[10] At the time, though, it was considered leading-edge theory.

Salovey and Meyer's concept of emotional intelligence emerged directly from Gardner's work. It was a subset of what had come to be known as "social intelligence," defined as "the ability to understand and manage people."[11] Emotional intelligence, they observed, was a specific skill set that included "the accurate appraisal and expression of emotion in oneself and in others, the effective regulation of emotion in self and others, and the use of feelings to motivate, plan, and achieve in one's life."[12] Emotionally intelligent people were special in that they were able to cue into feelings well, moderate their own and others' feelings, and use feelings—positive, negative, or otherwise—to help them get along in life.

Salovey and Mayer's notion of EQ as a set of skills didn't generate the kind of popular interest that Gardner's work had. Research psychologists accepted the emphasis on emotions in the conversation about intelligence, but the concept didn't really raise eyebrows beyond that. Outside of academia, the business world in particular was much more focused on "hard" skills like analytic ability, not so-called soft skills.[13] But that's where psychologist and journalist Daniel Goleman came in.

As a reporter covering science topics for the *New York Times*, Goleman encountered Salovey and Mayer's 1990 paper and reported later being "electrified" by the idea of emotional intelligence, which "offered a new way of thinking about our emotions."[14] His 1995 book, *Emotional Intelligence,* drew on their ideas, outlining five areas of emotional intelligence: alertness to our own emotional states; an ability to control or manage our emotions; our ability to motivate ourselves using emotion; empathy, or the ability to experience others' emotions; and managing others' emotions in the context of relationships.[15] Somewhat sensationally, Goleman argued that emotional intelligence "can be as powerful, and at times more powerful, than IQ," noting that "people who are emotionally adept . . . are at an advantage in any domain of life."[16]

Goleman's book struck a chord with the general public, becoming a massive bestseller and unleashing a torrent of popular interest that continues to this day. Everyone wanted to be "emotionally intelligent" because they were being told it was the real path to success in life and work. EQ put a label on something that we had been feeling for a while but were not able to identify: that empathy and emotions matter in life. In the workplace, it coincided with the bubbling over of long-held frustrations about gender inequality. Women are more emotionally wired than men, the thinking went, and the latter needed to start learning social and emotional skills in order to evolve. Goleman's book came out a few years after John Gray's hugely successful book, *Men Are from Mars, Women Are from Venus* (1992), and it could be argued that emotional intelligence accounted for the underlying difference in gender worldviews.

Time magazine ran a cover story on emotional intelligence, tantalizing readers with the notion that "emotional intelligence may be the best predictor of success in life."[17] Goleman elicited further excitement a few years later when he reported "research" (again, unsubstantiated and invalid) showing that "nearly 90 percent" of the gap separating "star performers" and "average ones in senior leadership positions" owed to emotional intelligence.[18] Others have made similarly striking claims, all of them unscientific. One company, for instance, claimed that people who score highly on their test for emotional intelligence earn $29,000 more annually than those who score low on it.[19] Shockingly, there were no links provided to that actual research, and it does not appear to actually exist. Again, the claims outweigh the science.

Energized by such proclamations, a thriving industry arose around emotional intelligence during the late 1990s and early 2000s that continues to flourish today. An onslaught of books and articles appeared on the subject. Psychologists developed tests to measure EQ, and consultants peddled frameworks and coaching exercises to help business leaders become more emotionally adept. Meanwhile, high-profile corporate leaders trumpeted emotional intelligence as pivotal to business success. General Electric CEO Jack Welch had a reputation as a tough, even ruthless boss who didn't mince words—on the face of it, not necessarily a poster child for emotional intelligence as most people think of it.[20] Yet he apparently came to hold the concept in considerable esteem. As he wrote in a 2004 opinion piece for the *Wall Street Journal,* "No doubt emotional intelligence is more rare than book smarts, but my experience says it is actually more important in the making of a leader. You just can't ignore it."[21]

Today, emotional intelligence is ubiquitous in the workplace. I see it everywhere: from companies requiring employees to take EQ training courses to executive coaches trumpeting the centrality of EQ in leadership. Many professionals receive training in emotional intelligence at work—one 2019 survey found that 42 percent of companies offered it to their senior leaders.[22] Other studies have found that a large majority of employers regard EQ more highly than raw intelligence.[23] *Harvard Business Review,* of all places, published a 2018 book excerpt describing Abraham Lincoln's emotional intelligence in leadership.[24] I remember seeing a tweet about this at the time and nearly lost my mind: How the heck could anyone ascribe emotional intelligence as described in the research literature to Abraham Lincoln?

Emotional intelligence haunts me everywhere in my work. When putting together job descriptions, executive recruiters now almost always list emotional intelligence as one of their desired leadership characteristics. They often are just trying to reflect what their clients are requesting. When my own clients talk to me about who they are looking for before I assess a candidate, they almost always tell me that they're looking for someone who is strong in emotional intelligence.

And the influence of emotional intelligence has penetrated well beyond business. Observers have put it forth as essential for success in practically any form of human endeavor. Parents and teachers apparently need it.[25] So do athletes.[26] And doctors.[27] And police officers.[28] Not to mention investors, accountants, and actuaries.[29] Without much evidence or analysis, observers also turn to emotional intelligence to explain high performance of all kinds. Aside from Lincoln, George Washington was apparently strong in emotional intelligence, as was Martin Luther King Jr.[30]

Such hype around emotional intelligence is understandable. The concept has a ring of common sense to it. All of us have known and liked people who seem emotionally sensitive and empathic. These people, generally speaking, tend to be more pleasant to be around. (But remember, empathy and "niceness" are not EQ as defined by Salovey and Meyer!) We've also all had bosses or colleagues who seem devoid of emotions—we know what *that's* like. For most of us, emotional intelligence is also an appealing concept on its face. It's reassuring to think that it isn't just the brainiest among us who succeed in life—nice guys and gals also finish first precisely by virtue of their niceness. In my practice, I've heard countless parents describe their kids as follows: "My oldest, he's brilliant, top of his class. My daughter? She's not as traditionally book smart, but she is *emotionally* intelligent. She has EQ rather than IQ."

If such ideas sound like so much wishful thinking, rest assured, they are. The popular concept of emotional intelligence *sounds* great, but below the surface, you find that it's largely bunk. Bear in mind, it's not just me saying that. A number of other psychologists have expressed doubts about the popular notion of EQ, including Salovey and Mayer themselves, the concept's original proponents. In a 2008 journal article, they and a coauthor observed the resonance of the concept both within academic psychology and the wider culture, writing that "the apparent size of the field dwarfs what we regard as relevant scientific research in the area."[31]

What about the evidence purportedly showing the practical value of emotional intelligence for leaders, managers, and other professionals? Salovey and Mayer have critiqued contentions by Goleman and others that EQ can account for extraordinary performance,[32] and many other scholars have offered strong critiques as well.[33] Reviewing the available evidence, John Antonakis, a professor of organizational behavior at the University of Lausanne, concludes that researchers "have been long on claims but short on evidence regarding [EQ's] utility for leadership."[34] What evidence does exist is "flimsy," failing upon analysis to meet basic scientific standards. Elsewhere, Antonakis concludes that evidence supporting the notion that emotional intelligence matters for leadership is "nonexistent or very weak at best and contradictory at worst."[35]

You don't need to be a research psychologist to understand that emotional intelligence might not adequately predict enhanced performance. An anecdotal glance at successful leaders past and present suggests as much. Some hugely successful leaders seem quite strong in emotional intelligence. Microsoft CEO Satya Nadella jumps to mind, having spoken passionately about the business and shown a willingness to express a certain amount of emotional vulnerability.[36] But we can also find no shortage of notable leaders who were "hard" people seemingly insensitive to others' emotions. In his study of superbosses who not only built powerhouse businesses but also helped others around them to succeed, Dartmouth professor Sydney Finkelstein suggests that some were prototypically hard-driving bosses who cared little about the feelings of others around them. Focused on winning, these "glorious bastards," as Finkelstein calls them, usually didn't "seem as nice or empathetic as we might wish our bosses to be." A good example was Larry Ellison, founder of software giant Oracle, who claimed that early in his career he invented his own approach to management: MBR, or "management by ridicule."[37]

The problem isn't just the lack of sufficient evidence supporting the grand claims made on behalf of emotional intelligence. It's that the concept itself as it has evolved doesn't make sense from a scientific perspective. In their 2008 article, Salovey, Mayer, and a coauthor specifically criticized Goleman's depiction of EQ, presenting it as a "complex and, at times, haphazard composite of attributes" that they pointedly hadn't endorsed. They're absolutely correct. In their initial research almost two decades earlier, Salovey and Mayer had spoken of EQ as a set of skills and knowledge related to emotions. In 2008, they refined this definition but continued to represent EQ as a set of four skills: purposefully managing emotions to achieve objectives, understanding emotions and the language used to describe them, identifying the emotions that we and others feel, and enhancing our thought processes via emotions.[38]

Goleman's concept of EQ, in contrast, amounts to a hodgepodge of abilities/knowledge and innate traits. His baseless definition includes self-regulation and self-awareness related to emotions, which are abilities, but it also includes empathy and sociability, which are personality traits. It's important to understand—both in general and as you read this book—that abilities and traits are very different things. We can develop abilities by taking steps to cultivate them and to build our knowledge base. Think of general intelligence, a measurable level of ability and general knowledge. Salovey and Mayer conceived of EQ in the same way: some people have a certain set of abilities and knowledge specific to emotions. Conversely, personality traits are the building blocks of our character—they are ingrained attributes or tendencies that are largely beyond our power to cultivate. As originally defined, EQ was an ability, but Goleman corrupted it in such a way that it became a measure of personality. Add to that, Goleman's model includes a factor linked to motivation—a broader concept that is conceptually distinct from our emotional life.

Goleman and others who followed this thinking are working with a bastardized version of EQ. In their hands, EQ is scientifically incoherent and boils down to "being nice" or "a people person." Niceness is wonderful—I'm as much a fan of it as anyone. But its power as a psychological concept is limited. It's no accident that the tests psychologists have devised to measure emotional intelligence don't work very well. If you're a corporate leader and you're relying on someone's emotional intelligence score to determine whether to hire or promote them, you're probably not measuring EQ very accurately. That's because the tests themselves don't measure the phenomenon they claim to measure.[39]

As this last point reminds us, questions about the validity of emotional intelligence aren't just a matter of academic debate. They have real-world consequences. Few serious people today would make important professional decisions such as whom to hire or promote based on an astrology reading. ("I'm a Libra. Hire me!") Astrology is generally considered a pseudoscience. Yet many people *do* rely on this concept in their decision-making. Emotional intelligence might *sound* scientific, and experts of one stripe or another might trot out something that approximates data to back up their contentions. But it's an "invalid concept," as one fellow organizational psychologist has written, a vague grab bag of psychological concepts assembled together and wrapped up in an attractive package.[40]

It's not that the more limited kinds of emotion-related skills that Salovey and Mayer describe aren't helpful. They are. Evidence suggests that skills related to emotions can enable us to perform marginally better. But even if they do, this holds true only if we work in certain kinds of jobs, such as sales or counseling, where emotional skills play a pronounced role.[41] In many other jobs, awareness of emotions is completely inconsequential with respect to performance or leadership. And in still other jobs where emotions matter less (accounting or brain surgery, for example), emotional intelligence can actually hurt us, perhaps because paying attention to emotions distracts us from focusing on other, more salient parts of our work, such as quantitative analysis or objective, focused thinking. Further, as psychologist Adam Grant points out, emotional intelligence has a darker side, with emotionally adroit leaders sometimes using their skills not to inspire others but to manipulate them.[42]

Even if we restrict ourselves to Salovey and Mayer's notion of EQ as "emotional abilities," in no way does having these abilities set us up for guaranteed success in our work or personal lives. By pretending that it does and treating it as the basis of our judgment, we're liable to come to poor decisions, whether we're trying to choose a candidate to hire, a partner to marry, or a business partner to invest in. We'll focus too much of our attention on fleeting emotional states, presuming that this gives us the best window into how the other person will behave. As a result, we'll fundamentally misinterpret people, missing the essence of who they are. In seeking out emotional intelligence in others, we'll hire, promote, partner with, invest in, marry, or befriend the wrong people simply because they come across as sociable and "nice." Bear in mind, being nice is easy to fake. Who among us hasn't encountered someone who seemed gregarious and friendly but later turned out to be a total jerk? By basing important decisions about people on whether they seem nice, we risk being manipulated by people who in truth are anything but.

The concept of emotional intelligence has been popular for decades now. Conversations around the importance of empathy and consideration of others' feelings is everywhere. And yet this cultural shift doesn't seem to have improved the quality of decision-making in our society. Wherever you look, you find that poor judgment is endemic. Surveys have found that bad decision-making is widespread inside organizations.[43] Poor hiring decisions abound, and bosses everywhere across industries struggle to manage their teams well.[44] Meanwhile, about a fifth of all small businesses fail in the first year.[45] A majority of business partnerships appear to end in failure.[46] And although divorce rates have dropped, they still hover at around 40 percent.[47] Such failures depend on a multitude of factors, but clearly the discovery of EQ has not been a boon for good judgment. Many of us might have become more attuned to our emotions and more sensitive to others' feelings, but we're not making better decisions, and we're paying the price. Perhaps it's time for a different approach.

A DEEPER WAY TO UNDERSTAND PEOPLE

WHAT ABOUT FRANK, THE software entrepreneur who faced the critical task of choosing someone to run his company's core business? He needed to choose between three applicants, each of them very different and strong on paper. To choose well, he had to anticipate how each of these candidates would likely behave on the job and how that behavior would affect their performance. He'd select the one whose behavior would allow them to perform the best given the specifics of the job, the organization, the business environment, and so on.

How could Frank accurately predict these candidates' future behavior? His emotional intelligence wouldn't help him much here. What Frank needed to do to choose wisely was to understand key aspects of the candidates' *personalities*. That is, he needed to glean the aspects of their character—including their thoughts, feelings, and actions—that distinguished them from others and defined them as individuals.[48] Since these traits remained largely constant over time, identifying and understanding them could give Frank a fairly accurate sense of how the three candidates would likely behave on the job and which would do best in the role.

In the years ahead, Frank's core business would need to operate with more structure and scale methodically in order to keep delivering on customer needs. In this regard, Frank knew that the new leader he hired would have to possess a number of important personality attributes. They would have to be structured in their leadership and disciplined in scaling the business. Being organized and process-oriented would be important. At the same time, they would need to possess some core traits consistent with the company's culture, which was entrepreneurial, risk-taking, and growth-focused. In a scrappy market like theirs, this leader also would have to be action- and goal-oriented. They would need to know how to act decisively and get things done. Given the range of personalities within the company and the presence of people who were often smart and highly opinionated at the same time, this leader would have to be honest, transparent, a good listener, and flexible as a communicator—someone who could motivate different stakeholders and resolve disputes.

Candidates who possessed these personality traits in abundance would be more likely to succeed. To screen his candidates for these traits, Frank could consider their past work experience and education and try to infer their personalities from that, in effect using the résumé as a proxy for personality assessment. If a candidate attended an elite college and excelled there, Frank might be able to glean that they were smart or diligent. If a candidate had worked at or led start-ups before, Frank could presume that they possessed an entrepreneurial spirit. If they had made some unusual career moves, Frank might have thought that they were risk-takers. But the problem is that people are more than their résumés, and despite what you've been told, past experience is not the best predictor of future performance.

To determine who would be the best fit for the role, Frank might also cultivate a special skill of his own; namely, the ability to observe these candidates during well-designed interviews and other interactions and come to his own, scientifically backed assessments of their character. This ability to understand the uniqueness of individuals is what I call *perceptivity*. And as we'll see, it's a wonderful superpower to have as you navigate your personal and professional life.

Think of perceptivity as a bundle of different skills related to personality. At its core, perceptivity is the ability to understand and name personality traits, recognize them in others and oneself, infer how traits affect behavior, and make good decisions as a result of this knowledge. John D. Mayer, one of the chief proponents of emotional intelligence, uses the term *personal intelligence* in a similar manner. He suggests that it has four distinct components: First, you must be able to read personality well in others and look introspectively to glean who *you* are. Second, you must develop ways of thinking about personality, giving names to certain traits and recognizing how certain ingrained models of personality you have might be influencing how you perceive others. Third, you must become skilled at making decisions grounded in your understanding of your own personality. And fourth, you must become skilled at framing broader life goals for yourself based on the person you understand yourself to be.[49]

THE SCIENCE OF PERCEPTIVITY

ALTHOUGH YOU MIGHT NOT have heard of perceptivity, the idea that we can have a kind of X-ray vision into others' individuality is not new. Since antiquity, philosophers, theologians, and others have developed theories of character and temperament and sought to discern various personality types.[50] The Greek philosopher Theophrastus elaborated an early system of personality types, naming thirty different kinds of characters, including "the suspicious man," who "believes that everybody is fraudulent," and "the thankless man," a Debbie Downer type who always sees the glass half empty.[51] Influenced by the theories of the Greek physician Hippocrates, medieval thinkers thought expressions of personality were related to some mercurial mixture of bodily fluids (blood, phlegm, and bile).[52] Later, during the seventeenth and eighteenth centuries, physiognomists such as Giambattista della Porta and Johann Kaspar Lavater advanced the idea that you could discern someone's character by studying their external appearance. (The latter notion persists in the popular expression "stuck up"— that is, the presence of a nose lilted upward, meant to signify that a person had an arrogant personality.)[53] Of course, this pseudoscience was completely unsubstantiated. Over time, it proved wildly wrong and often racist.

During the late nineteenth century, the modern science of psychology began to generate powerful new insights into personality and its expression. Since then, psychologists have focused on answering two basic questions: First, what is the true nature of the human mind? And second, what differentiates people from one another? The first of these questions led Sigmund Freud, Carl Jung, Karen Horney, Carl Rogers, and many others to study aspects of personality that all of us share, including the nonconscious mind, the mechanisms by which we engage in various behaviors, and so on. The second of these questions led scholars to first describe and measure differences in general intelligence and to posit that individual traits serve as the fundamental building blocks for the expression of personality.

During the early twentieth century, scholars began using statistical analysis to identify and isolate specific personality traits—what became known as the science of psychometrics. Adopting a linguistic approach, they began cataloging all of the terms that describe people—words like *curious, kind, open-minded, generous, extroverted*—and determined mathematically which of them defined distinct personality traits and which of them clustered together to form a single trait. The words *organized* and *tidy*, for instance, were not psychometrically distinct: Someone whom we might describe as organized would also be tidy, and vice versa. But someone who is organized might not be generous, and vice versa—those two traits are distinct.

I'll have a lot more to say about the psychometric approach and the pathbreaking insights into personality that it has produced in the next chapter. For now, it's important to note that our current understanding of personality traits and their expression is grounded in decades of painstaking research and analysis. This work has also given rise to sophisticated tests that allow us to reliably identify personality traits in people. I'm not talking about those fun, breezy quizzes in popular magazines that allow you to figure out if you or your significant other is a certain "type." Nor am I talking about popular tests like Myers-Briggs that, as we'll see, lack any real scientific basis. I'm talking about carefully designed and rigorously tested questionnaires that quantitative analysis has shown to measure what it purports to measure and to do so accurately. Most tests of emotional intelligence don't stand up to serious scrutiny. Scientific tests related to personality, however, do.

You might wonder: Are personality traits actually as real and enduring as psychologists think? After all, people behave differently in specific contexts. If we're chatty and outgoing at dinner parties, that doesn't necessarily mean that we'd consider ourselves an extrovert. At work, we might feel intimidated and clam up. Noting the unevenness with which people express certain traits, some psychologists during the mid-twentieth century argued that our personalities are situational at their core and not essential parts of us.

While the science ultimately refuted this point of view, psychologists have gotten better at acknowledging the complexity of personality and how it manifests in real-life situations. A consensus now exists that possessing certain personality traits *increases the odds* that we'll behave in certain ways in a given situation, but it doesn't guarantee it—other factors make a difference, too. It's kind of like a weather forecast: the chances of rain might be high, but what actually happens remains to some extent an open question. If we're extroverted by nature, we'll probably feel inclined to chat with people at parties, while standing in line at the grocery store, or when meeting neighbors on the street. But we'll also have times when other factors—we're sleepy and feel grouchy, we're upset about something, we feel intimidated—cause us to turn inward and become avoidant. Personality traits help us greatly to predict behavior, but they're no guarantee that someone will act in a certain way at a certain time.

PERCEPTIVITY AND PERFORMANCE

PSYCHOLOGISTS HAVEN'T CORNERED THE market on having insight into other people. We all practice perceptivity as we go about our lives. "With luck," psychologist David Funder has written, "you might go many years without being assessed by a psychologist. But there is no chance whatsoever that you can long escape being assessed by your friends, enemies, romantic partners—and yourself."[54] Evolutionary science suggests that we all have at least some innate perceptivity to draw upon that we inherited from our distant ancestors. In particular, behavioral scientists such as Steven Pinker, David Buss, and Leda Cosmides have shown an evolutionary link between present-day human psychology and prehistoric human psychological need. One area of this research revolves around *social cognition*, the psychological muscle of processing, storing, and using information related to our social environment. Within this context, we can connect behavior such as interpersonal aggression, mating behavior, disease avoidance, power and status, affiliation, and family connection back to prehistoric human survival needs.[55] Judging who is a friend or foe, and making decisions based on this insight, has long been a factor in the survival of the fittest. In a similar way, sizing up others also allowed our hunter-gatherer forebears to get along better with one another and to collaborate in ways that improved chances of survival.[56]

Beyond the innate perceptivity of human beings generally, you might wonder if some people today innately outperform others at spotting personality. Most people think they are better judges of character than everyone else. (Of course, that statement is statistically impossible—read it again.) For years scholars cast doubt on this notion, regarding perceptivity as more a learned skill than a natural ability. However, recent research into what is called "the good judge" of character suggests that some people do have an advantage in this area. One 2019 study found "consistent, clear, and strong evidence that the good judge does exist"—in other words, some people are indeed better than others at judging personality.[57]

My own experience bears out this finding. Over my two decades of working with leaders across industries as wide-ranging as private equity, apparel, health care, and agribusiness, I've found that some people are extraordinarily adept at judging others, but these individuals are few and far between. The vast majority of professionals *think* their judgment of others' personalities is accurate. In truth, they fall prey to a whole range of biases that skew how they size people up and in turn lead to horrible decision-making.

Evidence suggests that how good we are at judging people matters, significantly influencing how we perform.[58] Research psychologists have successfully demonstrated that accurate readings of personality "are important not only for specific professions but also for positions within every organization." Such readings allow managers inside companies to hire the right people and to provide feedback that will most likely resonate with workers as individuals. They also allow people to make better decisions about whom to trust, whom to interact or collaborate with, and whom to approach with new ideas.[59] Since numerous studies have linked various personality traits with strong job performance, and since those linkages are statistically quite strong, it stands to reason that an ability to spot these personality traits in others affords us a big advantage.[60]

I've seen this advantage play out in my own work when it comes to specific decisions that leaders and managers must make. When clients of mine have assessed others poorly or haven't even bothered to try, they've almost always lived to regret it. And when they've gleaned others' personality well, they've made stronger decisions that have paid off handsomely.

Frank is a good example of the former. Unsure of which candidate to choose, he asked me to help him assess their personalities—in effect, to partially outsource his own perceptivity for the purposes of making his decision. I conducted a psychological assessment, collecting considerable data about the three candidates. I had them take formal personality tests and conducted deep-dive, one-on-one interviews with each of them. As described in the introduction to this book, this specially designed interview probed the candidates' histories and underlying personalities. It enabled me to understand the nuances of who these candidates really were.

In the end, I concluded that each candidate had impressive character strengths, but they also had aspects of their personalities that made them ill-suited to the specific job for which Frank was considering them. One of the candidates revered authority and as a result would never stand up to Frank and raise objections when he needed to. Two were strong strategic thinkers but didn't have the temperament required to dig into the details and operate a complex business day-to-day. Such a temperament would be critical for the role—the successful candidate needed to be an operator, not a strategic visionary like Frank.

Ultimately, I concluded that none of these candidates were suitable for the job, and that Frank would do best to continue his search. Frank wasn't exactly thrilled to hear this feedback. He had already invested significant time and energy assessing these three candidates, and he wanted to make a decision quickly and move on. Against my recommendations, he wound up ignoring my analysis entirely and picked one of his three original candidates, the strategist who had worked at a big tech company and whom Frank had personally mentored. Predictably, the choice backfired. As I'd warned, this candidate, exceptional strategist though he was, struggled to manage the business day-to-day and couldn't get his team to execute at a tactical level. He just wasn't operationally focused. Important priorities fell through the cracks, causing disarray within the company. Within a year, Frank fired him and replaced him with someone else.

In other situations, integrating personality insights into decision-making has allowed leaders and companies to achieve great outcomes while working through incredible challenges. At one large law firm we work with, one of the senior partners—I'll call him David—was abusive, causing grave problems for the organization. On one especially egregious occasion, he spat on a colleague in the lobby of the firm's office building, in full view of many (if any one of them had recorded it and put it out on YouTube, it would have gone viral overnight). Others within the firm wanted David fired on the spot. The inconvenient truth was that he was a very effective attorney and a huge breadwinner for the firm. If he left, some of the firm's highest-profile and most lucrative clients would leave as well, rendering the firm a shell of its former self.

Human resource managers at the firm brought me in to try to understand what the hell to do with him. More formally, they were asking whether the firm might resolve the problem without having to fire the partner. At first, HR told me it was an issue of emotional intelligence and that this should be the focus of any intervention. I explained that emotions are just part of the story and that to really help I needed to determine which underlying personality factors might be a factor. They agreed and I conducted a psychological assessment of David, which included my deep-dive interview and some formal psychometric tests to gain insight into his personality. My assessment confirmed that he possessed many traits that allowed him to be successful as an attorney. He was energetic, engaging, persuasive, bold, comfortable with risk—all very helpful for a high-powered lawyer. He also lived by a strong moral code that guided his behavior and caused him to be protective toward those he loved.

My assessment also revealed that he had an anxious, impulsive, and at times combustible personality. If David felt even remotely slighted, he would blow it up in his mind and react explosively. He was ambitious and relentless in his pursuit of success, but in some situations, his passionate nature would manifest as aggression, his anxiety as moodiness, his impulsivity as a failure to consider the consequences of his behavior. He became irritable under pressure, anxious about his performance, and his moral code led to stubborn inflexibility, worsened by a need to always be right. He was a perfectionist, and when things weren't perfect or just in his mind, he reacted. These aspects of his personality could make it very difficult for David to get along well with colleagues. When triggered, he had a tendency to lash out—just like he did that day in the lobby.

As I told David and his bosses, he couldn't magically erase these negative aspects of his personality—they were as much a part of who he was as his more adaptive traits. What he could do was become more aware of his behavioral tendencies and take steps to correct or balance them out. In other words, he could do the work to develop a level of personal maturity he didn't yet have. It wouldn't be easy and it wouldn't happen overnight. He needed to understand the nuances of his personality as well as the internal issues he was grappling with and the parts of his own history that had helped form him. If he did that, he could develop strategies for moderating his negative tendencies. He wouldn't be able to eradicate his bad behavior entirely, but he might well be able to reduce the frequency and severity to the point where it was much less disruptive to others.

It's not easy in corporate contexts for problem employees to agree to go to therapy, but happily, my message resonated with David. The initial insight he gained into his personality thanks to our testing made a difference; namely, that it helped him to acknowledge behavior patterns he hadn't fully understood and to grasp ways in which his natural tendencies sapped his effectiveness at work. He started to see a therapist and made important progress within a few years. He was able to control his negative impulses while retaining important expressions of his personality that had long contributed to his success. Instead of leaving the firm, he now thrives there, leading to an improvement in the broader work environment.

In David's situation, it again wouldn't have sufficed to have focused on emotional intelligence—that would have shed light on just a small portion of the problem: emotional regulation. It would never have revealed his deeply rooted issues with authority or his relentless pursuit of perfection and underlying justice mentality. It wouldn't have convinced him of the need to go to therapy and delve deeper into who he was as a person, why his character had developed as it had, how the same traits that led to his success also led to destructive behavior, and how he might consciously adjust his behavior and thinking to moderate the expression of his underlying traits so that he could be more of the person he wanted to be.

To understand people, you need to know more than just their state emotions, those fleeting feelings and how they're expressed. You must understand the building blocks of who they are as people—their personalities. You need to know how they think, how they interact with others, what motivates them, what trait emotions (e.g., a "happy person") they possess, and how they work. Overemphasizing EQ when hiring is a fool's game. You might think it helps to understand the emotions of candidates when you interview them for a job. I'm not so sure. Skillfully understanding candidates' emotions could tell you whether they feel nervous, sensitive, or excited in the interview. You could see how they manage their anxiety in the moment, and you might understand your own emotional reaction to the candidates. What you won't know is how candidates will likely behave *after* the interview is over, including once they've reported in to work. You'll be clueless about who they are, and you'll potentially mistake their fleeting emotions for predictable, stable traits.

BECOMING MORE PERCEPTIVE

GIVEN THE LINKS BETWEEN perceptivity and performance, you might wonder if you can improve your ability to observe others and grasp who they really are. The good news is, you can. Moreover, improving perceptivity will make you a better judge of character and a better person for it. Studies have found that good judges of personality tend to be more relationship-oriented, agreeable, and positive-minded than others.[61] But even if we don't happen to naturally possess those traits in abundance, we can still cultivate specific skills, habits, and tendencies that allow us to take the measure of people as individuals. We can learn more about the workings of personality, understanding how individual traits give rise to specific behaviors. We can sharpen our thinking about traits, developing an extensive, personality-related vocabulary we can use to distinguish subtle nuances of individual character. We can practice observing behavior in the moment, becoming more adept at teasing out the underlying character traits it represents and becoming more aware of our own biases as observers. We can look inward, examining our own core traits and how they influence our behavior.

Becoming more perceptive might seem like a daunting task, but you can make progress more quickly than you think. Over the course of my twenty-year career, I've developed a simple method that my team and I use every day to help our clients improve their perceptivity and infuse everything they do with keen character insights. This method is grounded in the science of personality, leveraging the subdiscipline of psychometrics I mentioned earlier and tapping into easily applied aspects of long-held practices within psychodynamic psychology. At the heart of this method is an extraordinarily useful "cheat sheet" you can use to quickly size up a person and make more informed decisions about whom to select, how to build and manage relationships, how to optimize your own performance, and how to influence others in the moment.

To be clear, utilizing this tool won't give you a perfect picture of yourself or anyone else. But like the X-ray machine in a doctor's office, perceptivity can give you a picture that is sufficiently detailed and accurate to be practically useful in your day-to-day life. Perceptivity affords you a huge advantage over the surface-level shortcuts and stereotypes people typically use when sizing others up. Seeing beyond race, religion, socioeconomic status, political beliefs, and other superficial characteristics, you can understand core character and make better people decisions based on it.

Imagine how startling and empowering it must have been for doctors when they saw an X-ray for the first time. It would have changed their whole perspective on the human body. My cheat sheet—this book—aims to do something similar with interpersonal relationships. As you learn about perceptivity and begin to use it, you'll find that it utterly changes the way you understand and experience individuals and their behavior. New dimensions of conduct jump sharply into focus, all because you now have a structured, informed way of looking at them. You can make helpful predictions about how people you meet are liable to behave, in turn allowing you to make better, more fruitful people decisions.

Good judgment isn't what you think. It entails understanding the full spectrum of who we are as individuals, not just our fleeting emotional life. In the chapters ahead, we'll explore how to do just that by developing, disciplining, and honing our powers of social observation and interpretation.

KEY INSIGHTS

- If you're relying on emotional intelligence to help you make better people decisions, you're in trouble. Popular notions of EQ are bunk.
- Another, more profound approach to judgment *is* backed by science: perceptivity, or the ability to understand and assess human personality.
- Popular proponents of emotional intelligence have bastardized a scientific theory that does have merit but is of limited usefulness when it comes to exercising judgment.

- Personality traits are real and consistent, and they influence our behavior. It follows that being able to spot certain personality traits can help us predict how others will likely behave. In turn, we can make better, more informed decisions in situations where people are involved.
- We can improve our ability to glean our own and others' personalities. The key is to radically change how we judge.

Chapter 2

THE PERSONALITY BLUEPRINT

WHEN I WAS A junior in high school, my friend Michelle invited me to her house to celebrate her birthday. It was a small gathering—just five or six kids. I knew everyone except for a couple of friends from another high school whom Michelle had met that summer. One of them, a girl named Eva, caught my eye. I found her incredibly attractive—not only was she pretty, but she also had a certain happiness about her as well as a sparkle of mischievousness. Although she seemed quite a bit out of my league, I mustered the courage to make small talk with her.

Imagine my surprise and delight about an hour after I returned home when Michelle called to say that Eva really liked me and wanted me to call her. I played it cool, but inside I was pumping my fist in the air and shouting, "Yes!" I called Eva and we ended up talking for hours that same night. Something was clicking, but I had no idea what it was. The next day, Eva showed up at my high school just before lunch to hang out with Michelle, but in reality I knew she was there to see me. I got a chance to show her around and later have lunch with her and a bunch of our friends. Although I still barely knew her, she seemed like a lot of fun, the kind of person I'd enjoy hanging out with. My seventeen-year-old's hormones were running wild.

I was generally oblivious when it came to girls, but this time I took the hint and asked her out. We wound up going out for dinner later that week. This was my big opportunity to size up her character and see if she was "girlfriend" material. I did what most of us would do when we're trying to get to know someone, asking questions, listening intently, and at the same time trying to sound interesting and engaging in return.

But as Eva sat across from me and I attempted to get a true sense of who she was, I found myself overwhelmed. There were so many subtleties to pay attention to from minute to minute: the details she recollected in her stories, the wording she used, the way she carried herself, the opinions she held, the cultural references she made, the tone of voice she took, the food she ordered, the clothes she wore, the facial expressions she adopted—the list went on and on.

The next day, a buddy of mine asked how the date went. I found myself in a state of confusion. Although I liked Eva and felt great chemistry between us, I couldn't get a clear picture of who she was as a person. I call this state of being overwhelmed in social situations the Too Much Data problem, and it bedevils anyone seeking to gain quick insight into others' character. On any given occasion, so much information comes at us so quickly that we can fail to arrive at any clear insights. Other factors might also hamper us from observing and interpreting personality traits accurately. If we're distracted or tired, we might be even less capable of paying attention and sifting through the data flowing at us.

The obvious solution is to take our time getting to know other people, observing them over multiple interactions and in a variety of settings, and also getting feedback about their personalities from others who know them. I was fortunate to spend time with Eva on a number of other occasions over the following weeks. She showed up to my school the next day (a very good sign!) and we hung out. We went out for dinner, saw an awesome Rolling Stones concert (after which we kissed for the first time), went to the movies, spoke way too long on the phone, and much more. As these encounters played out, we learned more and more about each other—and liked what we had learned. As still more time passed, we started a relationship, fell in love, broke up for a while, got back together, and eventually got married. Thirty years and three kids later, we're still together.

In many work situations, we don't have the luxury of getting to know a prospective colleague, employee, customer, or business partner in slow, incremental ways. A brief interview or lunch meeting is all we get. Even when we're dating, most of us want to form judgments about our dates as quickly as possible so that we don't waste time pursuing a potential relationship that either won't happen or won't work for us. How might we more quickly glean other people's core personality traits—what makes them unique as individuals—from what they're saying or doing? Is it possible to get to know someone well enough to make important decisions with confidence from just a few social encounters?

Experts suggest all kinds of helpful questions we might ask to make the most of job interviews, dating situations, and the like.[1] But such advice is usually haphazard, ungrounded in science and impractical. And just the fact that we have a set of questions in our back pocket when we enter a social interaction doesn't mean we'll be able to make sense of the flood of data—some useful, some not— these questions unleash.

What we need is a new lens onto social interactions, a way of interpreting information about people that allows us to bypass the complexity, quickly focus on what's important, and ignore what isn't. Such a lens exists. As we saw in Chapter 1, scientists have used statistical techniques to pinpoint a few basic groupings of core traits—key dimensions of personality—that allow us to describe people and accurately predict their behavior. Researchers vary in their accounts of the precise number of core traits, but a dominant model has arisen that distills personality to five dimensions.

I've devised my own version of this model in my work, one that I find more relevant and easier to understand and explain. I call it the Personality Blueprint. I've fine-tuned and deployed this model to quickly and effectively assess thousands of people over the past twenty years. With my Blueprint in hand, you'll be much better placed to understand others and make high-stakes decisions about whom to hire, fire, promote, partner with, and more. We can also use the Blueprint to make big decisions in our personal lives, including whom to date or marry, whom to befriend, which nanny to hire for our children, and how best to manage these and other relationships.

The point of the Blueprint is to organize insights about others in such a way that will help you avoid the Too Much Data problem and thus understand the underlying essence of a person. Think about it this way: Have you ever tried to move tall, heavy piles of papers by grabbing each pile one at a time, holding it in your arms, and carrying it where it needs to go? Quickly you find that you're carrying too many papers and they begin to fall. It takes way longer to move such material loosely, so what do you do? You put them into large, cardboard file boxes. Once they're boxed up, you can do whatever you want with them easily and efficiently. Transporting them, categorizing them, arranging them, and ultimately making meaning from them becomes infinitely more manageable.

In a similar manner, my Blueprint won't give you an exhaustive list of ways to describe others whom you wish to assess. Human beings are much too complex for that, and it becomes unwieldy to even chase that objective. Rather than trying to track hundreds of disparate traits and compare people with one another on that basis, we can gain valuable insight into how individuals will behave by zooming in on just a handful of key dimensions. Organizing insights into figurative "boxes" corresponding to scientifically determined dimensions leads to a much more accurate and usable read on people. It affords us a whole new vantage point on the world, a kind of X-ray vision into other people that we can use to make shrewder, more reliable decisions. When it comes to exercising good judgment and achieving our goals, the Blueprint just might be the most important framework we'll ever have.

THE RISE OF THE "BIG FIVE"

BEFORE INTRODUCING THE BLUEPRINT, I'd like to take a moment to discuss its origins. I've related that the birth of psychometrics during the early twentieth century led to a seventy-five-year quest to uncover the true structure of personality, with scholars using mathematics and statistics to isolate personality traits. At first, these scholars focused on words, adopting what we now call the lexical approach to personality. Scientists reasoned that just as humans tended to pass physical characteristics down through the generations, so psychological characteristics must have also persisted through the words we use. To understand personality, we can analyze language, seeking out aspects of character that give rise to many descriptive terms in a given tongue—and that also are expressed *across* languages. The most important areas of difference among individuals, psychologists theorized, are those that have numerous synonyms, each articulating nuances in meaning, and those that are recognized by people in diverse cultures.[2]

Scholars amassed large lists of adjectives related to character—everything from "animated" to "zealous"—and began to isolate mathematically which of them actually represent distinct phenomena. Having people fill out surveys in which they rated themselves on a number of traits (and having others rate them as well), researchers performed statistical analyses to discover patterns as to which traits tended to go together. If you rated yourself highly on "extroverted," for example, an analysis might have revealed a very high probability that you would have rated yourself highly on related traits like "gregarious," "sociable," and "energetic." Similarly, it might have registered only a low or moderate probability that you rated yourself highly on other traits that seemed more farther afield, like "honest" or "smart" or "diligent."

Proceeding in this way, scientists sought to identify a relatively few, distinct groupings of traits that would give personality an underlying structure. As they put it, they sought to discern higher-order factors of personality—the broad categories of traits that define who we are. Working during the 1920s and '30s, a brilliant Harvard psychologist named Gordon Allport found that there were almost 18,000 words in the English language describing human character.[3] Organizing these traits hierarchically according to their significance, he posited that they make up the fundamental building blocks of personality, giving rise to individual differences in human thoughts, emotions, behavior, and motivations.[4]

The question among scholars became exactly how many higher-order factors of personality there really were. Hans Eysenck, a controversial British psychologist, theorized that only three primary categories of traits existed—he identified them as extroversion, neuroticism or "unstable emotionality," and "psychoticism" (the last of these a sort of witches' brew of several traits).[5] We should note that Eysenck postulated all kinds of dubious theories about personality during his career, many of which have been vehemently debunked. For instance, he believed that there was a "cancer personality" type, and he also proposed racist hypotheses around intelligence. Although Eysenck was deeply flawed as a person and his broader theories have been proven false, his three-factor model of personality enjoyed wide influence for many years.

Of course, other theories gained traction, too. In 1934, noted psychologist Louis Thurstone made a high-profile speech in which he presented research showing that personality "can be accounted for by postulating only five independent common factors."[6] Some work during the 1940s and '50s suggested that there were as many as sixteen factors.[7] Still, other research kept pointing to a five-factor model.[8]

By the mid-twentieth century, this line of research had yielded a confusing hodgepodge of models—a situation that unfortunately wouldn't change anytime soon. It was around this time that Sigmund Freud, the founder of psychoanalysis, introduced his famous theories to both academic psychology and the wider public market. Freud's perspectives on personality shifted the entire discipline toward the unconscious, addressing *why* people behave the way they do rather than just describing the nature of personality. His ideas were influential at the time but haven't all aged well. In particular, Freud has been ridiculed for his apparent overemphasis on sexual drives (the infamous Oedipus complex is pretty out there, and there isn't really evidence of its actual existence). Nonetheless, some of his core discoveries—that early experiences affect our personalities as adults; that unconscious thoughts and motivations drive behavior; and that we use psychological mechanisms to defend against psychologically harmful thoughts—were truly revolutionary and endure to this day. We actually owe a lot more of our understanding of people and their personalities to Freud than most current psychologists would like to admit.

Scientists during the 1940s and '50s were firmly focused on

popularizing tests that would allow psychoanalytically oriented psychologists to describe patients' personalities. In retrospect, some of these tests were pretty wild. The famed Rorschach test, initially developed decades earlier but popularized during this era, presented people with ambiguous inkblots and had them describe what they saw. Other such "projective tests" were developed, including the Draw-a-Person test (exactly what it sounds like—you draw pictures of people that psychologists then analyze) and the thematic apperception test (you look at an ambiguous image and describe the story you think it portrays).

Whereas quantitative surveys score personality against an objective norm or standard, projective tests are more subjective, prompting some psychologists to perceive them as less reliable and useful as guides to unearthing personality traits.[9] Notably, a number of psychologists have dismissed the Rorschach test as being essentially useless and even pseudoscience, despite its air of validity. "I would like to offer the reader some advice here," the American psychologist Robyn Dawes once wrote. "If a professional psychologist is 'evaluating' you in a situation in which you are at risk and asks you for responses to inkblots . . . walk out of that psychologist's office. Going through with such an examination creates the danger of having a serious decision made about you on totally invalid grounds."[10]

Although many of these tests lacked scientific validity, they proliferated in part because of the U.S. Army's need to evaluate recruits on their suitability for officer and other roles and in part because of the growing public popularity of psychoanalytic thinkers like Freud and Carl Jung.

Yet another important factor driving the rise of personality testing at the time was the proliferation of management consulting firms that sold business advice to corporations. The Hay Group, founded in Philadelphia in 1943, began using early personality tests in their consulting work, as did Rohrer, Hibler & Replogle, a Chicago company that became the first firm of psychologists that consulted to business leaders. (This second firm still exists, now called RHR for short, where I spent eight years on staff earlier in my career.)

Models of personality fell into relative obscurity during the 1960s and '70s as the discipline of psychology became skeptical of the very notion of traits, much less our ability to group them scientifically and assess them in others. As one scholar observed, psychologists had come to regard theorists of traits as "witches from 300 years ago," noting that "one is hard pressed to find one in the flesh or even meet someone who has."[11] During the 1980s, however, researchers began to dust off Thurstone's notion of five important factors of personality and to find evidence for it across a number of previous studies. Quantitative research by a range of scholars led to the consensus that we can reliably describe individual personality by focusing on just five supercategories of traits.[12] In 1996, psychologists Paul Costa and Robert McCrae published a seminal article on the topic reviewing decades' worth of research on personality traits and confirming what has become known as the five-factor model. In the years since, nearly all psychology researchers came to rally around this model. The "Big Five," as this framework has become known, is today about as close to a fundamental scientific law as exists in psychology.

What are these Big Five exactly? If you took personality psychology in college, you might remember the acronym that describes these dimensions of character: OCEAN. Openness to Experience (O) has to do with the extent to which you're creative, inventive, open-minded, or, on the contrary, more conventional-minded, rigid, and incurious. Conscientiousness (C) describes whether you're punctual, hardworking, and organized or constantly late, lazy, and disorganized. Extraversion (E) captures whether you're outgoing, active, energetic, and sociable as opposed to reserved, quiet, and a loner. Agreeableness (A) is about being generous, likable, good-natured, and trusting as opposed to stingy, irascible, and untrusting. Finally, Neuroticism (N) covers whether you're anxious, self-conscious, and emotional as opposed to calm, confident, and even-tempered.[13]

Each of these bundles covers much more conceptual ground than I've indicated, but you get the gist. We can regard them as "higher-order" factors because they are both independent from one another and the basic building blocks from which we can derive all other human traits. All told, these five factors capture what is most salient and important about an individual's personality. Any other words we might use to describe human personality ultimately will fit into one of these five higher-order traits. Moreover, if a personality test reveals that you rate highly in one of these five factors, that score suggests that you also will rate highly on all of the other, more nuanced traits that correspond to that factor.

Scientists also have found that your scores on these tests can predict with considerable accuracy how you're likely to behave in the future—good news for leaders and companies seeking a tool to help them exercise good judgment. Significantly, they've found that scoring high in certain areas—Conscientiousness, for example—correlates with higher achievement in some jobs and Agreeableness predicts it in others.[14]

During the early 2000s, Canadian psychologists Michael Ashton and Kibeom Lee proposed yet another model of personality, called HEXACO, that broadened the structure to include six factors.[15] The two scholars derived HEXACO using a similar lexical approach as the Big Five, with a twist: they also included non-English words. The sixth factor Ashton and Lee identified is called "honesty-humility" and encompasses traits like modesty and the avoidance of greed.

While HEXACO has generated some excitement in the field, personality researchers haven't been able to validate it consistently,[16] the model doesn't differ substantially from the Big Five, and we lack appropriate tests for measuring it.[17] For these and other reasons, few psychologists outside of academia use HEXACO, and the Big Five remains the most widely accepted model of personality.

WHY THE BIG FIVE AREN'T ENOUGH

IDENTIFICATION OF THE BIG Five was a major accomplishment in psychology, one that impacted society profoundly. Today thousands of consultants use personality tests based on the Big Five to probe people's character and help organizations make important decisions. Well-informed and effective practitioners prefer scientifically valid surveys such as the ones I've described in which people rate themselves on descriptive statements that tap into relevant traits. Other practitioners use poorly constructed tests not derived from the Big Five, including nice-sounding but invalid tests like the popular Myers-Briggs Type Indicator, DiSC, or CliftonStrengths. Still others use outdated projective tests—I know one company that remarkably still uses inkblot tests to select executives. American readers might be surprised to learn that some European companies actually hire graphologists to analyze the handwriting of potential hires to discern their character (pro tip: do not do this!).

Given my own background in personality assessment, I use Big Five–derived tests (some of which I will describe later in this book) in my own work with clients as one part of the assessment process. Indeed, my own doctoral research applied quantitative personality testing to a growing social disruption and what I believed to be a pending social problem. During the late 1990s, I conducted research largely focused on personality predictors of Internet addiction—the combination of personality traits and thought processes that could predict who might become addicted to the Internet. Administering personality tests and collecting behavioral pattern data, I demonstrated statistically that people low in extroversion, high in neuroticism, and low in conscientiousness were at risk of falling into patterns of excessive Internet use.[18] This made sense: People low in extroversion used the Internet as a social proxy, finding it easier to communicate with others online rather than in person. People high in neuroticism tend to have issues with impulse control, making it harder for them to stop once they've started to scroll. And people low in conscientiousness often procrastinate—surely connected to Internet addiction.

And yet, as decades of applied work since my days in academia have taught me, even the best tests based on the Big Five don't fully capture the totality of someone's personality. No personality test can capture the full complexity of human beings. It's one thing to understand whether a person has a given trait, quite another to know how that person will *express* that trait in their actual behavior, which is what we ultimately care about. I routinely encounter people who have similar personality profiles on a test but whose behavior is completely different. What accounts for that difference, I find, are the specific contexts in which people operate and the unique experiences that played a role in their growth and development. A generic test won't pick up these contexts and experiences. This is where the richness of psychoanalytic psychology comes into play. We are nuanced individuals who live unique lives. From my perspective, the Big Five provide the structure of our holistic personality, but our individual histories color the totality of who we are. Our personal journey is what makes each of us truly unique.

Remember David from the last chapter, the law firm partner

who publicly spat on a colleague? When given quantitative tests, he scored really high on the Big Five trait Neuroticism. His testing showed that he was prone to self-doubt, took criticism poorly, tended to react defensively, and could be irritable, moody, and hard to deal with. In the workplace, this part of his character inclined him (and uniquely him) to be very protective of his territory and to push back against any sign of aggression from others. He got into fights a lot, and beneath the tough exterior he was filled with self-doubt. At his core, he was needy toward others, always requiring their validation and becoming angry or upset when he didn't get it. He tended to lash out angrily at bosses and others in positions of power, seeming to nurse a seething resentment.

In a totally different context, I gave the same personality test to another individual, "Stuart," and he, too, scored high on Neuroticism. He was anxious and reactive toward others and took criticism poorly. But he didn't exhibit the same degree of dependency or neediness that David did, nor did he behave aggressively toward people in positions of power. Rather, he tended to respond in ways that were quieter, more avoidant, and more passive-aggressive. If you met him, you saw an uncertain person; a humble worrier who lacked confidence in his abilities and always seemed to see the downside in life. Two people, two similar test results, but very different behaviors that would affect how we'd size up these individuals when making important decisions.

Going beyond quantitative personality testing allows us to better understand this difference in their behavior. Conducting an extensive, deep-dive psychological interview with David, I learned that his personality was shaped by devastating physical and emotional abuse he experienced as a child at the hands of his overbearing father. Like many traumatized children, David learned over time to cope with his fears by fomenting a deep rage within himself. He was thus ready to lash out at the first sign of being slighted because the trauma he had experienced was still very much alive for him.

Stuart had also experienced childhood trauma, but of a very different kind. In an emotionally charged interview about his early years, he told a horrific story of family violence and abandonment. When he was a small boy, his father murdered his mother and was sentenced to life in prison. For the remainder of his childhood, Stuart went to live with his aunt and uncle, where he was largely left to fend for himself. He, too, emerged from this trauma quite anxious and reactive toward others, but it manifested itself as fear rather than rage. He was ready at any time for disaster to strike, fearful of what might happen if he upset people, and faint-hearted at any sign of emotions.

As this example suggests, we are more than our test scores. We are whole beings with complexities, nuances, and intangibles that a test simply won't capture. We each are a function of our experiences, our upbringings, the wider world with which we interacted as children, and the people we happened to come into contact with, all of which influence the narratives we craft about our lives. To truly understand others, we must understand these personal narratives, taking a more psychodynamic (another word for psychoanalytical) approach that recognizes the impact our early lives have on us. Instead of just quantitative ratings of people, we need qualitative categories that enable us to fill in the blanks.

These limitations of Big Five testing have enormous consequences. Many companies are content to test job applicants and decline to extend job offers solely on the basis of test results. Unbeknownst to them, they're only getting a partial read on how these applicants will likely behave on the job. As a result they are at risk of hiring the wrong people and passing over some very attractive candidates. Big Five testing can help orient us generally to the character of individuals, but to get a useful and accurate picture we must consider other data points. And the more significant or complex the decision at hand, the more data points you need to feel confident.

THE BIG FIVE AS AN INTERPRETIVE FRAMEWORK OR BLUEPRINT

TO GATHER ADDITIONAL DATA points, there's another way we can use the Big Five: not as the basis for a psychological test, but *as a qualitative framework to help us observe behavior and glean personality in real-life settings.* The Big Five can help us solve for the Too Much Data problem by giving us a mental template we can use in the moment to help us sift through the information coming at us. In other words, it's about organizing qualitative insights we have into people, not measuring or describing them. Rather than trying to take in random information about a person sitting across from us, we can focus our attention on just five broad areas of inquiry, sifting out relevant information and organizing it in our minds as it comes in. As we'll see in the next chapter, we can even ask questions aimed at teasing out information about each of the five traits. If we happen to see another person on multiple occasions but for shorter durations, we can also decide to focus each time on one of the Big Five to see what we uncover. By narrowing the scope of the information about others we regard as relevant, we can deepen our insight in the limited areas under our gaze.

Using the Big Five as an interpretive template during in-person encounters can help us to fill out some of what quantitative testing misses. During conversations, people reveal Big Five traits in their richness and specificity, often allowing us to tie these traits back to their context and personal history. Their speech and nonverbal behaviors *embody* traits directly—they're right there for us to experience. You don't get a number telling you whether someone is high or low in a trait. You see that trait coming to life in front of you, embodied in a unique way that we can describe qualitatively.

While writing this book, I happened to take a three-hour flight from Toronto to the fairly remote city of Winnipeg. Just before takeoff, the flight attendant informed us that we would be late taking off because a few passengers were running to make the flight. Twenty minutes later, these passengers came on board and one of them, a woman in her fifties, sat down next to me. Irene, as I'll call her, seemed somewhat frazzled, telling me that she had been in transit, had only booked a very short layover, and was grateful to have made it. She was quite talkative and animated, and over the next hour, proceeded to tell me her life's story—and then some. I learned that she was a nurse who worked in remote areas in northern Manitoba, that she had two sons in their late twenties, that she was having trouble with her finances, that she didn't care much for desserts, that she had enjoyed a recent vacation in the Dominican Republic but had gotten food poisoning, that her husband was a retired teacher, that some countries around the world had great educational systems but others didn't. She had a frenzied demeanor as she related all of this to me, speaking quickly and in bursts, waving her hands around, at one point nearly spilling her wine on me and then repeatedly apologizing.

I found Irene to be a lovely person, friendly and not at all offensive or overbearing. From a psychological perspective, our encounter was hugely revealing of her personality. When regarded in connection with the Big Five, her chattiness with me, a total stranger, revealed that she was high on extroversion. No headphones for her, she wanted to talk. Meanwhile, her late arrival, the fact that she hadn't planned her layover well, and her frenzied presentation all pointed to her low conscientiousness—this wasn't the first time she was late for something. Moreover, I sensed that she hated being late, even if she somehow always was. She signaled high neuroticism, as did the anxiety and intensity that caused her to speak quickly, go off on tangents, and cause her to nearly spill her wine on me.

Without realizing it, Irene blatantly exposed all of these personality traits to me in a short period of time. They were right there on the surface, ready for me to interpret. Further, they were there in a tangible form, expressed through specific language and bodily movements that linked back to elements of her context and personal history. All I needed was a framework that allowed me to pay attention in a certain way, separate the signals from the noise, and make sense of what I was seeing and hearing.

Used as such a framework, the Big Five serve incredibly well as something like a blueprint for character. An architectural blueprint is a plan for a building, an abstraction that helps us understand key aspects of how the finished structure will look. It provides a way of organizing the dimensions, appearance, and contents of each of the building's spaces. Let's say you have a blueprint of a new house you're building. With your blueprint in hand, you can go furniture shopping, figuring out what piece goes in which room. You see a sofa and you know that goes in the den, while that nice table goes in the dining room and that bed goes in the bedroom. The very structure of a house enables you to make sense of a store as you walk through it. Similarly, the Big Five when used as an interpretive blueprint doesn't measure someone's personality but rather enables us to organize and make sense of aspects of an individual's character. Understanding these dimensions of character, we're in the best possible place to make sound decisions about people.

Ultimately, using the Big Five as a blueprint serves as a way of disciplining how we engage in social interactions, allowing us to experience them in a way that better serves our purposes. Without such an interpretive tool, we might well pay attention, but we're not necessarily able to extract useful information about personality. As a result, we tend to bumble along, grasping scattered insights about others when we can but failing to probe very far into their characters. With the Big Five as our guide, we can quickly notice patterns in other people that help us anticipate how they will likely behave. The quality of our judgment improves in turn.

ADJUSTING THE BLUEPRINT

EARLIER IN MY CAREER, as I started to assess people and their personalities, I noticed something: the Big Five were scientifically valid and predictive, but they were also insufficient. They capture important information about a person's character, but not all of it. For instance, most of us would probably consider a person's motivations—including what they care about, what they perceive is important in life, how religious they are, whether they are driven by money and fame, how much risk they're willing to take, how ambitious they are, and so on—as an important and even defining part of their character, but the Big Five doesn't capture motivational traits.

Likewise, our intellectual capacities—not just how smart we are, but what kind of thinkers we are, how we make decisions, how strategic or tactical we are, whether we are skeptical or philosophical or theoretical or practical—also help to define who we are as individuals. Again, these are insufficiently captured in Big Five tests, which measure Openness to new ideas but not how a person really thinks, or how good they are at solving problems. I also took issue with some of the language of the Big Five, finding it too cumbersome, out-of-touch (try telling a layman that they are high in Neuroticism), and difficult to explain to clients.

Bothered by these shortcomings, I modified the framework I was using to glean personality in social situations. I wound up crafting one that, although based on the Big Five, was tailored more specifically to generating information helpful in making practical decisions about people. I call this framework the Personality Blueprint (**Figure 1**).

A PRACTICAL BLUEPRINT FOR JUDGING CHARACTER

Box #1: Intellect—How People Think

Box #2: Emotionality—How People Express Emotions

Box #3: Sociability—How People Engage with Others

Box #4: Drive—Why People Do What They Do

Box #5: Diligence—How People Get Stuff Done

Figure 1: The Personality Blueprint

I use the word *box* here to describe each category of information because I want you to literally think about putting information about people into one of these boxes. Imagine these boxes stacked up in this order from left to right. When you meet someone and they reveal something about who they are, mentally put each insight that comes at you into one of these boxes. Now, you may say, "Wait, Richard, are you telling me to put people into a box?" To that I reply: No, don't put people into a box; put them into *five* boxes.

Let's run through each of these boxes in a bit more detail. The first, Intellect, describes the manner in which people process information, make decisions, and solve problems. When trying to size someone up, it's critically important to understand how smart they are in a traditional sense, how impulsive or restrained they are, how practical their thinking is, and how organized their ideas are. Is a person analytical or more intuitive? Are they decisive? Are they focused? Are they thorough? How fast and accurately do they process ideas? Are they worldly and global in their mindset? Are they creative? What is their tolerance for risk? Can they handle ambiguity? Are they capable of flexibility in their thought? The Intellect box covers qualitative information related to personality traits (including those found in the Big Five Openness to Experience factor) and general intellect. It should help you capture someone's problem-solving, thinking, and decision-making capabilities.

The second box, Emotionality, is similar to Neuroticism in the Big Five, describing the extent to which trait emotions affect behavior. Note that I'm not talking here about how emotional people may be when you meet them, but rather how they tend to typically experience or express their emotions. Some people lead with their emotions and wear their heart on their sleeves. Some deal with stress by suppressing emotions and detaching themselves from the issue and others in general. As an aside, an entire body of research within psychology called attachment theory holds that people's handling of their emotions often reflects their early attachment with parents or authority figures.[19] Those of us who grew up in loving, caring homes tend to show warmth and emotional maturity. Those who grew up with cold, distant parental relationships often suppress emotions or seem detached themselves. Finally, those of us who grew up in unpredictable, emotionally charged environments tend to show evidence of erratic, emotional immaturity.

To understand people, it's extremely important to determine how they go through life emotionally. What is a person's typical mood (are they a happy person or a downer)? What happens to them when stressed or in a crisis? How sensitive or defensive are they? Are they resilient and hardy or do they break down easily when challenged? Are they confident in themselves? Are they patient with others? Are they self-conscious or confident in who they are? Are they anxious and tense by nature, questioning themselves or seemingly paranoid about everything?

The third box to consider when trying to glean someone's personality is Sociability, or how they tend to engage with others. Combining Extroversion and Agreeableness from the original Big Five, this category addresses communication, interpersonal capabilities, and how someone gets along socially. To understand a person, it is essential that we capture how they come across to others—the words they use, the interpersonal impact they have, how sociable and gregarious they are, and how effective they are in communicating their thoughts. Is a person authentic and sincere? How skilled are they in social situations? Are they expressive? Are they tactful? Are they good listeners? Are they verbose or concise? Do they have a commanding presence or more of a meek or subtle one? Do they talk with elegant sophistication or uncomplicated plain-speak? How well do they do when communicating spontaneously? Do they engender trust in others? Do they fit in easily and conform to groups or are they independent and get into conflict with others a lot? Do they form relationships easily and manage them well?

Fourth, consider Drive, or why people do what they do. To really understand someone, we must understand what motivates their behavior. You may be motivated primarily by money or fame, while I may be motivated by the chance to exert influence or to serve the community. The more I understand what impels you, the better I am able to adjust my approach in dealing with you. Are you ambitious? Are you altruistic and driven to help others? What are your perspectives on money, and how does it affect you? Are you motivated by creative expression, and will you feel stifled in a boring environment? How much initiative do you generally show? Do you give up easily or do you persevere? Which values drive your behavior? How would you characterize your moral code and your efforts to live by it? Finally, let's not discount your political leanings, as they do tell us something about you. Are you conservative, progressive, or something in between?

Finally, pay attention to a fifth box, Diligence, or how people get stuff done. Similar to Conscientiousness in the Big Five, this category encapsulates the habits and capacities a person has in relation to performing our duties at work and in life. Some of us have a highly structured, disciplined approach to life, while others of us are much more laid-back and spontaneous. Understanding someone's dispositional leanings will clue us in to what to expect from them. How responsible are they? Are they good at managing their own work? Can they manage their time appropriately? Are they well organized? How disciplined are they? Do they create systems for getting stuff done?

I've presented these dimensions as independent, but in reality they inform and relate to one another in interesting and important ways, coming together to help us understand the whole person. As an example, consider Elon Musk, arguably the most famous CEO of our time (although in my view far from the most effective). Based on what I've heard from people who've seen him in action and in reading Walter Isaacson's recent biography,[20] it's clear that Musk seems uncomfortable when engaging with others. But this social discomfort doesn't exist in isolation—it's closely linked to his way of thinking and to other aspects of his personality.

Musk is obviously a visionary and complex thinker, highly persuasive, and incredibly ambitious. He is also on the autism spectrum.[21] People with autism are often—but not always—socially awkward and lack a basic understanding of social conventions and people in general. They often have delayed language and movement skills that affect their ability to fit into social environments. They often are impulsive and tend to vacillate between inattentiveness and intense focus—in the blink of an eye, they can shift from grand ideas to minute details. They also tend to be moody and emotionally reactive. On the other hand, autism might also have given rise to some of Musk's extraordinary strengths, such as his creativity, attention to detail, and tenacity. My point here isn't to diagnose Musk but rather to show that personality traits are connected and can explain the behavior we see in others. We can use the Blueprint to understand specific traits, but these aspects of personality are also interdependent and paint a colorful picture of the whole person. A person's thinking style affects sociability, which affects diligence, emotionality, and drive, just as a person's emotionality affects intellect, and so on.

THE SIXTH BOX

WHEN DEPLOYING THE PERSONALITY Blueprint to judge people, we also should recognize that being high or low in specific traits isn't inherently good or bad. That depends on a number of factors, first among them the context in which you're operating and the behavior required of you. Musk's early involvement in PayPal and leadership at Tesla were historical feats of innovation and entrepreneurship. Interestingly, though, both of these companies were built around engineering (software in the case of PayPal, and both software and automotive in the case of Tesla). Musk's more recent acquisition, Twitter (now called X), is a social media company whose success depends on understanding people and social dynamics as much as code. Musk did an absolutely awful job of managing people during his early tenure as CEO of X, by many accounts impulsively firing employees and removing essential functions without apparent thoughtful planning. His personal tweets alienated users and advertisers alike, and he has suggested that he cares more about the power of his reach than the impact his tweets might have on X's business. Investors have taken notice: as of this writing, X's value has plummeted since Musk acquired the company, with users and advertisers leaving in droves.[22] As Musk's poor people leadership suggests, people are infinitely more complex than software or auto mechanics, and Musk's social deficits have impeded his ability to lead. Thankfully for X, Musk announced in May 2023 that Linda Yaccarino would take on the role of CEO. A psychological analysis of her public statements suggests that she is highly direct and assertive but significantly more collaborative and empathetic than her predecessor.[23] For the sake of X (a medium I have always enjoyed), I hope Musk stays out of her way.

Context is vital to consider if we are to understand others and come to nuanced judgments about them. Take Intellect. You might think it is generally advantageous to be able to understand complexity and nuance, but that's not necessarily true. To succeed in their jobs, senior leaders often must be strong strategic thinkers. This in turn requires that they possess a slew of intellectual capacities, including creativity, imagination, an ability to function amid ambiguity, and yes, an ability to understand business situations in all their complexity. But as many a failed CEO can tell you, it's possible to be *too* oriented toward understanding complexity. In many business situations, what matters most for senior leaders isn't the ability to generate big ideas but to take action and execute strategies. If leaders get carried away with complexity and feel compelled to think through every last nuance of a given problem, they can become paralyzed. Instead, they must translate strategy into specific tactics, zooming in on relevant details and forgetting the rest.

As I've found, individuals who are highly intellectual, complex thinkers often do well when they work as corporate consultants. That role rewards their ability to focus on the analysis and comprehension of a problem and its potential solutions. But these individuals struggle when they seek to transition into operational roles inside large organizations, which many of them do. As bright as these consultants might be and as much industry knowledge as they might possess, their personalities often lead them to prioritize vision and strategy when what the business really needs is the ability to execute the strategy tactically, communicate it to the organization, and motivate employees. On paper these consultants look eminently qualified, but in practice they come across as overly intellectual or academic—too focused on theory rather than on the demands of real life.

Meanwhile, a person who tends to think more superficially and has trouble or isn't patient enough to grasp complexity can often be very practical in their thinking and have a good intuitive sense of how to handle specific situations. Rather than thinking theoretically, they have "street smarts." You might not want such a person to serve as CEO of a global company or as general of an army, where strategy and vision really matter, but you would wish to select them over other, more brainiac peers to run an operating division or lead a battlefield regiment. Likewise, if you're on trial for a criminal offense, you might prefer to hire an attorney who knows intimately how juries and judges think and how to connect with them rather than one who can make pathbreaking and intricately nuanced legal arguments that nobody understands or cares about.

As we saw earlier, the specific ways that individuals express their personality traits also help to determine if those traits are helpful or disruptive. Imagine, for example, that you've been tasked with selecting a new member of your sales team. Evidence suggests that a certain clustering of traits can indicate a propensity for success in sales. A strong salesperson will likely be comfortable with people, at least somewhat personable or credible, highly empathetic, financially motivated, and optimistic. Translating these traits into our Personality Blueprint, you would want to pay special attention to candidates' Sociability when selecting someone for your sales team. Optimism falls in the Emotionality box, along with empathy and social sensitivity. Finally, one of the hallmarks of effective salespeople is that they are motivated by financial reward (the Drive box). I sometimes call this "coin operated"—put the right amount of money in and you will get the desired results. In many roles, primarily commercial motivations do not predict success, but in sales roles that require a person to hunt for customers, it is essential. Understanding this, recognizing it when you see it, and knowing when to capture it in the Drive box will lead you to make better judgments about people.

With any individual, specific traits can translate into behaviors that are both positive and negative. People who tend to feel and express strong emotions can be difficult to have as colleagues. Maybe they have a lot of internal angst and require constant validation. They might be overly dramatic, constantly upset about some petty conflict. They might panic at the slightest setback. They might lash out angrily at others or become distractible when they're irritated or in a bad mood. They might become defensive when a boss or colleague gives them even mildly negative feedback. On the other hand, these very same people might also be able to wield their emotionality as a superpower to get results. Nurses do this at your bedside when they behave compassionately. Kindergarten teachers do this as well when they show patience toward a boisterous five-year-old. The very emotionality that holds them back at some times also proves a valuable asset during others.

So much rides not just on the specific traits people appear to express, but on their ability to *master* whether and how they express them in everyday situations. When using the Personality Blueprint, pay attention to whether someone possesses the self-knowledge, maturity, and discipline required to anticipate and compensate for the less helpful parts of their ingrained tendencies, or if they can fine-tune how they express their traits to conform to the demands of a given situation. This self-insight and ability to master our own ingrained traits is so important that I regard it as a sixth box.

If someone is highly sensitive and emotionally expressive, do they let their emotions get the better of them in stressful situations, or have they learned how to contain their emotions in these moments? If someone is a highly abstract, conceptual thinker, do they know to compensate by surrounding themselves with colleagues who are more tactical and street smart? If someone tends to have a "salt of the earth" persona, are they aware of it and can they turn it on or off depending on whom they're with and the goals they're pursuing?

Our stable personality traits and how we express them shape our destinies in life, but that doesn't mean they determine everything. We still enjoy an important degree of agency. We can decide to push back against our latent tendencies if we wish, disciplining ourselves to behave differently and developing workarounds. I'm not suggesting that we should mistrust who we are and try to be someone else; "faking it" in specific situations to get ahead can leave us frustrated and burned out, even if it works in the short term. Rather, we should embrace who we are but also try to be our *best* selves, incrementally moderating our behavior to account for our limitations. The best performers in any field do precisely this, taking responsibility for the parts of themselves that aren't so attractive and striving to improve them. And the best judges of character take into account not just the core traits they observe in others and how those are expressed, but the extent to which others can moderate and channel their ingrained tendencies in desirable ways.

YOUR NEW SUPERPOWER

USE THE PERSONALITY BLUEPRINT to gauge the character of others around you quickly and efficiently, giving yourself an edge in your decision-making and relationships. With data about personality organized into five core boxes (and supplemented by the sixth box), you will have a powerful "cheat sheet" you can deploy to evaluate people about whom you need to make a decision. Sorting information into the boxes is actually an easy and worthwhile practice. Think for a moment about your spouse or a close friend of yours. Try and mentally fill the boxes in your head with everything you know about that person. Keep pressing yourself to fill more of each box. After only five minutes of doing this, I'll bet you'll have arrived at a highly accurate and succinct way of describing them.

Likewise, if you take a minute to think about your own habits, you'll be able to understand your own defaults relative to others and fill each box with personality insights about yourself. That's the power of the Personality Blueprint. It's nothing less than a new way of structuring what you see as you move through the world and interact with others. It's a way of instantly orienting yourself in social contexts, just as paying attention to basic features like topography, climate, and culture might orient you if you were plopped down into a new locale. Such an orientation will prove invaluable when you're trying to make quick but important decisions about people, manage relationships, develop a career trajectory, handle conflict, and much more.

Whether we realize it or not, we already apply mental frameworks to help us judge people. These frameworks, which might arise out of unconscious assumptions about racial difference, social class, or ethnicity, are riddled with biases and other problems. They don't predict behavior very well, nor do they allow us to make shrewd judgments about people. By contrast, the Personality Blueprint really works. Spend just a bit of time applying it in real-life situations and you can get very good at spotting behavior that fits into one of the five boxes. You also learn to ask questions of others that can reveal aspects of these five boxes to you. You can determine quickly and accurately how to categorize your insights about others and get a sense of how each of the five boxes manifests in their behavior. You can gain keen insight into people, catching patterns that most others miss and making better decisions on the basis of those insights.

Over time, using the Personality Blueprint will also help you to develop a more extensive vocabulary to describe individual differences. We all have a basic set of terms at our disposal that we can use to describe others—words like *kind, thoughtful, ambitious, competitive,* and so on. But you might not have an expansive enough vocabulary to capture important nuances and shades of difference. For instance, in seeking to convey that someone is not only sociable but also fun and enjoyable to be around, you might describe them as "outgoing." But other words might allow for even greater accuracy—terms like *affable, amiable, congenial, gracious, good-humored, jovial, cheery,* or *pleasant.* Each of these terms captures just a bit of added nuance, helping you to pinpoint more accurately a person's unique character. As you accustom yourself to observing others and using the Personality Blueprint to structure what you see, you can pick up new words to describe specific traits, experiment with them, and add them to your repertoire. Your perceptivity will improve in turn.

Once you understand the Personality Blueprint, the next step is to explore how precisely to mobilize it in specific situations to gain an advantage. The chapters that follow will help you to deploy the Personality Blueprint to select the right people and opportunities, to set relationships up for success, to optimize your own performance, and to influence others.

Before tackling these subjects, we must first take a deeper look at the more basic task of using the Personality Blueprint in conversations. Formal personality tests administered by professionals shed light on who people are, but as we've seen, a good conversation helps even more—if you know how to navigate it. Unfortunately, most people don't. They enter conversations hoping to get to know others, but they wind up blowing the opportunity, leaving with very little in the way of useful insight. By mobilizing the Personality Blueprint in specific ways, you can become far more skillful at the art of conversation, unlocking a wealth of information about others that you scarcely knew existed. With this new insight at your disposal, you'll be well on your way to exercising good judgment.

KEY INSIGHTS

- The Too Much Data problem makes it difficult to gauge another person's personality during encounters with them.
- As decades of scientific research have shown, we can assess personality in terms of five primary bundles of traits—the so-called Big Five.
- In addition to using formal tests to glean Big Five traits, we can

use this framework in another way: as a powerful template we can use to understand and interpret others' behavior.

- An adaptation of the Big Five, the Personality Blueprint assesses character by discerning five categories, or boxes, of traits: Intellect, Emotionality, Sociability, Drive, and Diligence.

- When interpreting personality, it's vital to consider what we might regard as a sixth box: Mastery, or the extent to which a person is aware of the other five trait bundles and can shape their behavior to moderate unhelpful dimensions of their personality.

- Mobilizing the Personality Blueprint, we can develop perceptivity as a new superpower, arriving in turn at better people-related judgments. Not only can we get better at spotting specific traits in others; we also gain a vocabulary that allows us to register fine-grained nuances in character.

Chapter 3

THE SECRETS TO
REVEALING CONVERSATIONS

IN 2017, I ATTENDED a meeting of the Under Armour apparel company's executive team. About a dozen highly experienced leaders sat around a huge table in a fairly traditional, wood-paneled boardroom, discussing the company's product strategy. The company had done incredibly well in recent years, consistently notching double-digit revenue growth, but lately sales had slowed. On this day, as the executives gave their presentations and pitched their ideas, the energy in the room seemed to wane. The presentations soon became a slog and the pitches, in many cases, were downright boring.

I thought the tone might shift as the conversation moved to one of the company's bright spots, its SpeedForm Apollo line of running shoes. Launched in 2014, these shoes were both interesting and innovative: Under Armour had worked with a women's underwear manufacturer to design them and had outfitted some models with tech, allowing runners to compile data about their performance.[1] Yet even this new topic couldn't shift the drab and dreary mood.

The firm's billionaire founder and then CEO, Kevin Plank, wasn't about to tolerate a boring meeting. Sensing the lack of energy, he became increasingly animated and at one point started to wax eloquent about what made the company's products special. Under Armour, he argued, couldn't sell just another pair of sweatpants or sneakers like anyone else. Each product sold had to express a purpose and elicit an emotion—*passion*. His voice rose as he said this, and his eyes flashed with excitement.

Then Kevin did something completely unexpected. He leaped onto the boardroom table to model the Under Armour footwear and clothing he was wearing. Strutting back and forth with his hands on his hips as if he were a high-end fashion model on a Paris runway, he said, "You see, these aren't just any shoes. These shoes have a purpose. Our apparel *means* something. We make athletes better."

The gesture was both shocking and entertaining—I would kick myself later for not filming it. I had never seen a CEO (or anyone really) leap onto a boardroom table before, nor for that matter had I seen one mimic a fashion model. I suspect nobody else in the room had, either. The mood of the meeting changed instantly. Everyone laughed and joked, and the subsequent conversation became much looser and more creative.

I had already assessed Kevin (in a somewhat unusual way at his home over a bourbon and cigar) and understood how people were drawn to him. But when I saw him leap onto that table, I understood the full extent of his leadership presence and how it served him in his business dealings. Here was a guy who could bend people toward him, influencing them through sheer charisma. His personality was hypnotizing, exhilarating, almost magnetic. He was confident, an iconoclast, and a risk-taker, a person who didn't hesitate to let out his emotions even if it meant violating conventions. He was also what we might call strategically empathetic, able to sense the emotions of others and respond in ways designed to achieve a desired result.

Most people in our lives don't put their personalities on display as colorfully and transparently as Kevin did that day. Some people even seek to hide their personalities out of fear, shyness, or a desire to please. When we speak with them, they might stick to superficialities, project traits they think we want to see, or ask questions so that *we* do most of the talking. Given such evasions, how can we manage conversations so that they reveal the most about people, whether it's someone we know well (a boss or a childhood friend) or a stranger we've just met (a first date or someone trying to sell you a car)?

The quality of our conversations has suffered in recent decades, thanks primarily to our near-constant immersion in communications technologies.[2] It often seems hard to focus on what someone is saying for more than a few seconds without becoming distracted, much less staying present long enough to discover deeper insights about their character. As we bury our heads in our phones, we can become utterly oblivious to what is happening around us. In recent years, authorities in Seoul, South Korea, have installed ground-level streetlights in the curbs of busy street corners because screen-toting pedestrians were getting hit by cars. Placing streetlights at ground level allowed pedestrians to see them while they were looking at their screens.[3]

All of this raises the question, how can we compensate for all the complex and vital social information we're missing as we stare at our screens? We can't. Indeed, many of us don't even try to engage with others face-to-face anymore. We prefer to conduct important conversations—breaking up with people, asking for raises, telling people that we love them—via text or email.

When it comes to judging personality, it's not enough to simply pay more attention. We must focus on the specific task of gathering data about others, asking questions that will induce people to reveal themselves to us, and reacting to what they say in ways that encourage them to disclose even more. To do this well, you need to have a psychologically driven strategy, making use of the Personality Blueprint described in Chapter 2. In the course of interviewing thousands of people across backgrounds and professions, I've developed a set of five powerful conversational strategies incorporating the Blueprint that allow us to elicit a wealth of data about personality and turn that data into useful insights—all without making our interaction seem clinical or overly evaluative. Deploying these strategies during even the briefest encounters, we can build relationships and walk away with the understanding we need to make far better people-related decisions.

STRATEGY #1: BUILD RAPPORT AND GET THEM TALKING

TO DRAW OUT TRUE personality, you must get people to trust you enough to speak openly about their lives. You can build this trust by engaging in a conversation that from the outset feels natural and normal, not stiff or forced. No matter what kind of relationship you have with the other person, put them at ease right away so that they feel comfortable divulging information and don't feel like they're under a microscope.

When I'm meeting someone for the first time, whether as part of a formal interview or in the course of everyday life, I first try to find a point of connection. I might mention the name of a person whom we know in common, or identify some part of my background that is similar to theirs. If a person happens to mention that they're a hockey fan (I live in Toronto, after all!), I'll relate that my kids play hockey, and we'll probably talk about the Maple Leafs. If they mention that they just endured a horribly long plane ride, I'll commiserate with them by describing a travel snafu of my own. To accentuate my message of friendliness and interest, I use my body language, smiling, offering an outstretched hand, turning my body to face the other person, looking them in the eye to embrace their presence. Each of these behaviors helps others feel welcomed and relaxed, making it more likely that they'll open up to me.

Building rapport and seeking out common ground might seem obvious, but many people underestimate it or don't know how to do it. In clinical psychology, this rapport building is called the "therapeutic alliance." Psychotherapists have long known the importance of creating this cooperative relationship with clients. In the workplace, people often ignore rapport building when conducting interviews. This includes people in my own field, professionals doing similar selection-assessment interviews.

About fifteen years ago, I was invited to interview for a job at a competitor firm. I flew to New York and met with one of the firm's senior partners at a Manhattan hotel. Entering the windowless meeting room, I braced myself for a three-hour meeting I assumed would be similar to the ones I conduct with my own prospective clients. I sat down and almost immediately the partner began grilling me on my life history. No tee-up or chemistry building, just straight into the interrogation, like he was a detective and there was a lamp shining brightly in my face. This interviewer was gruff and arrogant, and he kept his laptop screen up so that it separated us physically and psychologically. The interview was highly scripted and the conversation—if any—entirely one-sided. The whole experience felt cold and off-putting, as if this firm simply wanted to extract data from me and didn't care about truly knowing who I was or if I was a good fit. Ironically, they got less data out of me in those three hours than they might have. While the interviewer learned a great deal about the events of my life, he in no way understood me or my personality. Quite the contrary, he probably got me entirely wrong. Not only did I decide not to work for that firm; I left the interview convinced that there was a better way of learning about others that would help in decision-making.

Sharing a bit about yourself in the course of a conversation lends itself to finding common ground, further encouraging people to talk about themselves by establishing a precedent for self-disclosure in the conversation. We tend to set ground rules during the first few minutes of our encounters with others, sending subtle cues about how we're feeling in the moment and what kind of conversation we're open to having. If we clam up about ourselves, we're suggesting that voluntary disclosure is unwelcome, out of bounds, or otherwise a low priority. If we volunteer just a bit of personal information about ourselves at the outset, we convey to the other person that it's safe to do so, if they feel inclined. Our openness gives others permission to be more open, too.

We don't want to go overboard with our own self-disclosure, of course. If our goal is to gain insight into character, our primary objective during a conversation should be to get the other person talking—and to keep them talking. In the course of disclosing small bits of information about ourselves, we should quickly and deftly turn back to asking questions and showing curiosity. But again, this curiosity shouldn't be aggressive, as if we were investigative journalists or detectives following a lead. We must convey to the other person that there is no power structure at play here—that we are just ordinary people, with our own normal lives, trying to get to know them better.

One technique my colleagues and I use when beginning conversations is to first focus on the present context. Don't ask about the future or the past; instead, get people talking about their current activities. In a work context, that might mean asking someone about their role—what they like and don't like about it, the kinds of experiences they've had, what their current boss is like, how meaningful their work is, and so on. Outside of a work interview, the questions you ask will vary depending on the setting. Let's say you need to negotiate with someone in customer service, for example at a bank or retailer. Instead of going right to the issue at hand, spend a few moments asking questions to get to know them. Talk about how busy things seem and ask how they are coping. Ask "How is business?" or "Have you worked here for a long time?" The point is to get them talking in order to build that alliance. Then you can ask them the hard questions.

Such questions should convey genuine interest on our part. This again might sound obvious, but it is essential to make people feel that we are on their side, members of their team, and not adversaries sitting in judgment of them. To understand people better, we must become students of behavior. That means not only observing behavior but wondering *why* it occurs. It means regarding every interaction as a valuable opportunity to understand just a little bit better not just how the person in front of us ticks, but how people in general do.

If such curiosity doesn't come naturally to you, then my advice is simple: Ask more questions. Of *everyone.* Throughout your day, make a habit of leading with questions. When you interview contractors to build an addition onto your house, don't simply inquire into their past experience or their pricing. Get personal. Ask them to tell you something about themselves. How did they get into being a contractor? When did they discover they liked doing this work? Did they grow up building things? As you listen to the answers, think about asking deeper questions to follow up. It might feel odd at first to show so much curiosity, but with practice you'll soon find that avid questioning becomes a treasured (and impressive) habit.

STRATEGY #2: GET THEM TO
GLANCE BACKWARD

ONCE YOU'VE SUCCEEDED IN getting the other person talking, steer your questioning—and periodic self-disclosures—with an eye toward eliciting the most information possible about their personalities. The best way to do this is to get people talking about their personal story.

As I've mentioned, we're a function of the experiences in our lives, the sum total of our personal journey and the decisions we've made along the way. Personal stories provide a window into the self well beyond the core traits described in the classic Big Five model. By hearing someone's life story, you can not only learn about the kind of person *they* think they are but also understand how their personality has been shaped. If personality is who we are, it didn't come out of nowhere. While genetics may play somewhat of a role in personality, experience is the stuff it's really made of. We know from developmental psychology that identity is typically formed in our adolescent years and that it adapts over time.[4] Yes, we change and grow, and we are different from who we were back in high school. But that was the starting point, the dawn of our core personality. Consequently, if we ever want to know something about someone, we need to understand their earlier years and the story of how they lived out their lives. In this way, we can understand the distinct way people have made sense of their lives, integrating experiences into a coherent whole.[5]

A client of mine recently described the powerful influence his father had on him during his childhood. He explained that his dad tended to be quite impatient, and that he inherited this trait of his—he wants everything done *now*. He described a couple of recent instances when he became angry with others who in his view were moving too slowly. But he also noted that he isn't a replica of his father. Whereas his father tended to be quite guarded emotionally, keeping his true feelings hidden behind a veneer of masculinity, my client judged himself to be much more like his mother, who tended to be more expressive, sensitive, and free-flowing in her communication.

My client went on to describe a time in high school when he embarrassed himself by crying in public. He said that his close friends know to expect hugs and sentimental gestures from him—it's a running joke. At the same time, he's learned to tone down his emotionality in his professional life, projecting it only when it serves his purposes (such as when he's trying to motivate his team members or convince them to take a course of action). All of this discussion of the past provides valuable evidence about who my client is now—both his own impressions of his personality and behaviors that actually express specific traits.

If we have significant time to spend with someone—say, during a date, an extended job interview, or a cross-country plane ride—we might be able to get a fairly well developed, chronological sense of their life. But even during a shorter conversation—say, during a ten- or fifteen-minute chat at a cocktail party or on the sidelines of a high school soccer match—we can gain a surprisingly detailed sketch that provides valuable information.

If we're meeting someone for the first time, we might say, "So tell me about your journey. How did you get here?" Asking someone a basic question like "So, did you grow up here?" and then following up with additional queries can also get them started talking about their childhood. Again, the point here is to keep your questioning casual, striking a tone of friendly curiosity. We might also briefly explain the motivation behind our asking. In a dating situation, we might say something like "You know, I'd really like us to get to know each other better. Tell me your story—how did you get to be the person I see sitting across the table from me? People sometimes say that our past influences us in powerful ways, and I'd love to understand how that's been true for you."

In many everyday contexts, it might seem artificial or overly clinical if you ask for a blow-by-blow account of someone's childhood, education, and adult life up to a certain point. You can take a looser approach, asking a variety of questions that collectively will yield a coherent life story and in turn unleash a torrent of information about personality. You might ask them what it was like for them growing up, what their siblings were like, how they experienced high school, who some of the biggest figures in their lives were. Did they have a nice group of friends? What were they like? What college did they go to and why did they make that choice? How did they come to their present career? Did they ever spend time in a foreign country? What were they doing there? The list goes on and on.

As you ask these questions, begin the process of mentally categorizing the answers you receive, looking for evidence of specific traits and filing them according to the structure of the Personality Blueprint (more on this later). When I heard my client tell me that he had issues with patience, I could regard that as a piece of evidence suggesting that he was in fact impatient and aggressive in pursuing goals, mentally placing that bit of information in the Diligence box (Box #5—How People Get Stuff Done). When he told me that he tended to be more emotional and sensitive, that he once embarrassed himself by crying in public, and that his friends all joke about his sentimentality, I could mentally place all that evidence in the Emotionality category (Box #2—How People Express Emotions).

If you already know a person's basic history, you might decide to set aside questions probing the past and instead pose queries that focus in on specific Personality Blueprint categories. Or you could take a hybrid approach, delving into the other person's past while also op-portunistically lobbing questions that prompt them to reflect on their tendencies and behaviors here and now. Below are some of my favor-ite questions to ask relating to the Personality Blueprint dimensions.

STRATEGY #3: ASK POWER QUESTIONS

WHEN IT COMES TO exploring people's pasts, some questions are so effective in eliciting clues about personality that I almost always use them, particularly during short encounters when I want to max-imize the amount of data I collect. I call these power questions, and there are four of them. If you want to improve your judgment and wonder what to ask during your next date or interview, you can't go wrong with these particular four.

The first of these questions (actually a question accompanied by a follow-up) is one that yielded that earlier example of my client and his impatient father. I ask people to think of someone who was an especially big influence in their lives—usually a parent—growing up. Then I deliver the follow-up: "How are you similar to this person personality-wise, and how are you different?"

This question works because it knocks people slightly off-kilter. Most people I meet have never been asked this question, so it comes as a bit of a surprise. When thinking of similarities and differences, they might be tempted to speak critically about their parents or other influential figures, and they're often not quite sure that they should. At the same time, most people want to respond truthfully, especially if you've done a good job of building rapport and estab-lishing trust. Think about it yourself for a moment: How are you similar to your mother or father? How are you different? I'll bet the answer reveals a lot about who you are.

Box #1: Intellect—How People Think	1. How did you do in high school/college academically? What were your strong subjects and what were your weak ones? 2. What sorts of books do you read or podcasts do you listen to? 3. Did you play any music instruments or have any artistic abilities growing up?
Box #2: Emotionality— How People Express Emotions	1. What does it look like when you get stressed? 2. What are your hot buttons? What gets you frustrated and sets you off? 3. What is the hardest piece of feedback or advice you've ever gotten? What was your immediate reaction to the feedback?
Box #3: Sociability— How People Engage with Others	1. Did you have a lot of friends growing up or a few? Tell me about your social life back then. 2. Did you ever have to do public speaking when you were younger? What was it like for you? 3. What are your "friend turnoffs"? That is, what traits in someone make it impossible for you to truly be friends with that person?
Box #4: Drive—Why People Do What They Do	1. What do you love most about your work? What gets you up in the morning and excited about your day? What do you hate about it? 2. Who was giving you advice and support along your journey? Who have you leaned on for support and how have they given it? 3. Why did you choose your college major and ultimately your career of choice? What was it about them that fit who you are?
Box #5: Diligence—How People Get Stuff Done	1. How clean or messy is your office/house right now? What does it say about you? 2. Tell me about a typical day. How tied to your calendar are you? 3. Are you a detailed person? How do you deal with deadlines? Are you ever late for meetings?

Figure 2: Personality Blueprint Dimensions

Because this question is uncommon and forces the person fielding it to describe themselves *in relation* to someone else, the responses will usually be revealing. Or perhaps the respondent might start to offer an answer and then back away from it—also revealing. Perhaps the best thing about this question is that although it prompts people to reflect on their own traits, it does so somewhat indirectly, by asking them to think about someone else's character. Almost always, this question will prompt people to characterize themselves in certain ways in relation to others, and almost anything they say will reveal something interesting about them.

The second power question asks people to branch out beyond their parents or other key influences to think about their social context. "Think about your inner circle of friends," I say, "the core group, or if they aren't a group, your three or four closest friends. How would you characterize the people in this group? Do you observe any recurring themes?" You can also ask an opposing, more negative version of this question: "Let's say you meet someone new. You may or may not be able to work or get along with them, but something about them makes you feel that they wouldn't be a friend of yours. Kind of like a friend 'turnoff.' What trips you off to that?"

These questions usually prompt people to reveal their values to you (Box #4—Drive), without your having to ask them directly about what matters most to them in life. They also can yield a trove of other information. In describing their circle of friends, a person might relate that they are somewhat of a geek and hang around with other people who have strong intellectual interests. That might present some evidence that this person is curious and academically oriented (Box #1—Intellect). Or they might say that they have only a few close friends and don't go out much, but that their friends are deeply loyal, thoughtful, and committed. You might infer that this person isn't especially social or doesn't make new friends easily (Box #2—Sociability).

If you ask someone to describe the people they probably *wouldn't* wish to befriend, they might say that they don't feel comfortable around people who are too wild or flashy, or that they stay away from people who seem arrogant, or that they don't socialize with people who aren't up-to-date on politics or know what's going on in the world. Such responses might tell us about their motives and values (Box #4—Drive). Perhaps the person says they dislike hanging around people who are lazy or late all the time, canceling plans at the last minute. That might tell us about their approach to getting stuff done (Box #5—Diligence). Perhaps the person says they steer clear of people who appear insensitive or disloyal, not charitable or caring about those around them. That might suggest information about their emotional tendencies (Box #2—Emotionality).

A third power question I use is appropriate to pose only after the person has been talking about their history for a while. Let's say that they have told you a fairly detailed or interesting story relating to some past experience (college, a stint in the military, the year they spent studying abroad in high school, and so on). Rather than letting the story pass and moving on to something else, try asking the following: "If you think about your story, the one you just told me, how would you summarize or characterize it? If you could separate yourself from being the storyteller and think about the story itself, how would you describe the main character?"

The point is to prompt the person with whom you're speaking to reflect on their experience objectively, as if they were standing outside themselves. You might receive a response like, "This story is one about a kid who was pretty smart, not always the hardest worker, who struggled for years and finally found his way," or "This is a story about a girl whose parents gave her a raw deal but who, through hard work and focus, managed to make something of herself." Rather than you attempting to make sense of their past experiences and behaviors, the person with whom you're speaking can do that for you, pointing out their own character traits. They might validate suspicions you've had or point you toward traits of theirs you've overlooked. The shrewdness and sophistication of their response will also suggest their level of self-awareness, and it might also provide insight into the character and quality of their thinking—how analytical they are, whether they tend to see shades of gray or simply black and white, whether they tend to reflect on the past or are more oriented toward the future, whether they possess a great deal of raw intelligence, and so on.

A fourth power question asks the person to imagine what someone else they've known in the past would say about them. In a work context, this could be an ex-boss or a current coworker; in a dating situation, an ex-partner. "Tell me about your old boss," you might say. "If I were to reach out to that person, how would they describe you? What advice would they give me?" This question, like the previous ones, usually elicits an account of important character traits, which the person will either agree with or dispute. Often it will prompt people to reveal other information as well. Speaking of their boss, an employee might say, "She would probably tell you that I'm smart but not proactive enough and that I'm not a strong communicator. Bear in mind, though, that my boss is a little skewed in her judgment. She never liked me for some reason and doesn't know me all that well. She's also petty."

The person to whom I've posed this question doesn't know if I will really call their old boss or not. There is always that possibility—and maybe it's even a probability in a context like this.

It's the subtle psychological "threat" of this possible conversation that reveals so much. The question also serves us by eliciting information about how this person deals with others and with whom they typically associate. It helps us understand how reflective this person is and to what extent they have insight into their relationship with the other person.

In this instance, we might wonder if this employee really isn't proactive or a strong communicator. In that case, we might deduce that this employee has trouble receiving feedback, or that she struggles in her relationships with authority figures. We can't know for sure based on this response alone, but we can seek out other evidence that might point us toward certain conclusions. I often follow up this question by posing a similar one to this employee: What advice would someone else—a colleague or someone whom this person supervises—have for her? If I hear more defensiveness, that's revealing. If I hear advice that affirms the judgment of the employee's former boss, that's revealing, too.

These power questions are all fairly challenging, and they might put the other person in uncomfortable territory. At the very least, you're confronting the other person with queries that they probably haven't heard before, that require some serious thought, and that they can't easily weasel out of. Don't be afraid of a little awkwardness. It's okay to challenge people, so long as we do so in an open-minded way and from a place of genuine curiosity.

With each of these questions, we're not fishing for a particular answer. We're just trying to see how the other person will respond. An elaborate response will likely contain lots of data for you to unpack, but even brief, superficial responses, although less satisfying, might still reveal important aspects of a given personality, such as a limitation in their intellectual capability, a discomfort around certain topics, or a lack of self-awareness.

FOUR POWER QUESTIONS ABOUT THE PAST

1. How are you most like your parent (or other influential person), and how are you most different?
2. Think about your inner circle of friends in high school and beyond. What types of people are friends of yours? Can you identify certain themes?
3. If you think about the story of your life (or some other, particular story they just told), how would you characterize it?
4. If I called your old boss right now and asked her to tell me about you, what would she say?

Note: You can modify these questions to inquire about the person's present-day reality as opposed to the past. For example, "How are you most similar to and different from your mother?" or "Think of your friends today. What generally describes them?"

STRATEGY #4: PAINT A MENTAL PICTURE

NOW THAT WE'VE COVERED how to elicit information about personality, let's shift to the task of interpreting the data we receive. During our conversations, all of us are simultaneously collecting information from others, interpreting what we hear, and assessing others on that basis. Most of the time, we do this instinctively, without giving it much thought or even being aware of it. Much like the piles of papers and books described in Chapter 1, though, the insights remain loose, uncategorized, and difficult to actually do anything with. The Personality Blueprint allows us to interpret information much more deliberately, giving us a framework for recognizing and categorizing potentially relevant data.

As the person with whom you're speaking recounts information about their life, and especially about their past, note any details that might suggest a personality trait falling under one of the five categories in the Personality Blueprint. You might want to make actual notes on a piece of paper, dividing it into five boxes. I do this myself when conducting the more formal interviews described in Chapter 4. In the course of general interactions with people, of course, taking notes is impossible. That's no problem: get in the habit of mentally slotting details into the five boxes. This might seem difficult at first, but once you do it a few times, it gets much easier. **Figure 3** illustrates how you might interpret and slot some sample statements people might make in response to your queries.

Bear in mind, you can't simply conclude that a person possesses a certain trait based on the general information they provide. To feel confident in your judgments, you need multiple pieces of evidence that all point to the same conclusion. As you go along in your conversation, try to form working hypotheses about people and then confirm or modify as new information comes in. In **Figure 3**, the revelation that a person—I'll call her Lisa—left a well-paying accounting job they perceived to be boring in favor of a job in marketing that paid "peanuts" might lead us to surmise that Lisa is motivated more by a chance to live a creatively fulfilling life than by money. If we learned, for instance, that Lisa did a stint in the Peace Corps after college before taking a job in accounting, we again have evidence that money and the chance to build a lucrative career aren't foremost in her mind. If we further learned that Lisa is encouraging her own children to study art and music in college rather than more "practical" subjects and that she also enjoyed making pottery as a child and grew up with artistic parents, we can feel even more comfortable concluding that she cares most about expressing herself creatively, not achieving a certain level of financial success.

As you build these hypotheses, pose follow-up questions that help you confirm or modify the information you've received and your interpretation of it. Does your hypothesis continue to ring true

Statement You Hear	Possible Interpretation	How to Categorize It
"In high school, I was drawn to history—it just fascinated me to learn about the Middle Ages. I also loved fantasy books and sometimes I'd create my own."	Imaginative, creative thinker	Box #1—Intellect
"I feel quite confident about myself at work. I usually feel like I'm in control and don't question my judgment very often."	Calm, steady, not terribly neurotic	Box #2—Emotionality
"I've always loved working in an open office. I just love the camaraderie and the chance to collaborate with my colleagues."	Sociable, gregarious, collaborative	Box #3—Sociability
"I've always been the kind of person who needs to be constantly doing something new. I get bored easily. I left a really great, well-paying career in accounting to pursue a marketing position at a start-up because I just needed more energy, more novelty. I got paid peanuts, but I was finally happy."	Motivated by a chance to be creative, not necessarily by money	Box #4—Drive
"After college, I backpacked through Europe with a friend. We had no plan, no itinerary . . . we just went. I've always preferred to be spontaneous, figure things out on the fly, and roll with the punches."	Laid-back, spontaneous, not overly rigid	Box #5—Diligence

Figure 3: Interpretation of some sample statements you might hear in the course of conversation

given the new pieces of data that come your way? Maintain a certain amount of skepticism about what you're hearing, recognizing that others have their own agendas. When Lisa first tells us about her decision to leave accounting, we might wonder if she really does value money but is embarrassed to admit it because of her upbringing, for example. Only as other details emerge can we conclude that creative expression really does motivate her more than money does. If we learned that, in fact, she didn't have the academic grades to make it in accounting, and if she told us that she counseled her kids to stay away from the arts and that her hobbies were all sports-related as opposed to artistic, we might wonder how important creativity really is to her.

Such synthetic thinking—in which we bring together disparate pieces of data and fit them together like puzzle pieces—is vitally important when interpreting personality. Whatever the context and your specific objectives, you're not simply trying to identify individual behaviors and associated traits. You're seeking to understand how those behaviors and traits fit together and what the practical implications might be.

I'll never forget the time I met a top sports leader whom I'll call Patrick, someone whom I admire and call a friend to this day. Asking him about his background over lunch, I learned that Patrick grew up in small-town America, and that his family circumstances were very humble. His raw intelligence allowed him to get into a top college, where he excelled academically. Following graduation, he enlisted in the navy. While there, he became a lieutenant commander and served his country with honor and distinction. He subsequently went on to earn an Ivy League MBA. During his time in graduate school, a well-known sports executive gave a guest lecture; Patrick approached him afterward to seek advice. This effort led to a job offer with a professional sports team. Early successes there led to a precipitous rise: he went from assistant manager of a pro football team to a leadership role in the league office. Only a few years after that, he was recruited to be CEO of a prominent NFL team.

Patrick's incredible story, which he related in considerable detail over a two-hour networking lunch, revealed a great deal about his character. Reflecting on his story, it was obvious that he was extremely bright (the Ivy League background provided corroborating evidence), capable of big, creative thinking, and willing to take risks. He had confidence in his ideas and was highly innovative in pushing them forward—all insights categorized in the Intellect box.

As confident as Patrick was, I gleaned that underneath the surface he always harbored a perception of himself as a small-town guy. He was extremely resilient in the face of challenge and felt great empathy toward others, although he didn't always show it (Box #2—Emotionality). Further, I experienced Patrick as friendly and personable, willing to do anything for his friends and close associates (Box #3—Sociability). Patrick was motivated purely by achievement—he kept pushing himself simply because he felt he *had* to succeed (Box #4—Drive). Patrick's military background confirmed my impression of a disciplined, structured personality. He was a work-hard, play-hard guy who could put his head down and get the job done when necessary (Box #5—Diligence).

At one point just before we ordered some dessert, I started to realize that all of these traits that had enabled Patrick's rise to a position of power also caused problems for him. In particular, his tenacity sometimes led him to dig in too much when advancing his ideas rather than listening to the ideas of others and seriously considering them. Patrick's perspectives might have been entirely correct, but he lacked the patience to work with people who didn't see things his way. Asking some follow-up questions, I learned from Patrick that his colleagues perceived him to be combative during meetings, and that some had even told him that they felt intimidated by him. Although his confidence seemed boundless to others, Patrick told me that he actually feels uncomfortable among the big-city elite. He felt like an outsider, and this affected his behavior. I concluded that Patrick would need to work on smoothing over these expressions of his personality if he were to reach his fullest potential.

STRATEGY #5: CALIBRATE AND REFINE YOUR HYPOTHESIS

WHAT YOU HEAR DURING conversations with others is only one form of data at your disposal. In interpreting personality, consider other forms of data and use them to calibrate your hypotheses. Five forms of supplementary data are especially important: the general presentation of those with whom you're speaking, including nonverbal communications; the physical spaces these people occupy; your own visceral reactions during the conversation; the knowledge you have of your own personal biases; and how people with whom you're speaking perceive their own traits.

When I first sit down with someone, I pay particular attention to their general presentation. How are they dressed? How do they carry themselves? How well read do they seem to be? What is their general energy like? How are they behaving? Do they formally shake my hand or do they instead slap me on the back or avoid all eye contact? Do they seem attentive to what I'm saying or do they quickly become distracted and check their phone? Do they meet my gaze or are they deliberately looking elsewhere? Do they speak quietly or loudly? Do they laugh loudly and often or are they more subdued? Do they arrive late for our meeting or are they on time?

These and other aspects of a person's general presentation certainly won't tell us everything we would want to know about their personality, but they can provide clues that we can then compare with other information we might glean. If someone professes to be calm and unemotional but presents as agitated and high-strung, we might not want to take this person's impressions of themselves as accurately portraying their character. If they claim to be sociable but avert their gaze, speak softly, and hold their bodies away from us, they might be more introverted than they claim. Alternately, perhaps they are extroverted in general but something about the situation at hand causes them to withdraw or appear tentative and uncomfortable. Cultural factors also are incredibly important. In some cultures, direct eye contact signifies disrespect, not introversion. Awareness of such cultural factors will help you interpret what you're seeing and how it fits the context.

A second source of supplementary data about personality is environmental. If our conversation happens to take place at a space maintained by the other person, such as their home or office, we can also look to how they decorate or maintain their surroundings for further clues about who they are. Zoom meetings are particularly interesting on this front, as we get a glimpse into people's home office or personal spaces. (We sometimes can get too much information on someone via Zoom meetings. I once met someone new via videoconference, and they had their camera set up in their bedroom. I will not go into specifics, but the background was . . . telling.)

Our impressions of physical surroundings can serve as a fairly reliable indication of underlying personality traits. A profusion of photographs on an office wall or desk might suggest that a person is high in Sociability. The presence of an "I Voted" sticker might suggest that someone is socially conscious and offer clues about Drive.[6]

If we've judged a person to be highly organized and structured based on their account of themselves but their office is a complete mess, with papers and files strewn about haphazardly, we'll want to probe into it more. If their office is decorated by numerous pictures of their family, we might take that as evidence of their self-professed orientation toward family and home, or of a tendency toward sentimentality. If they have many pictures of themselves standing with famous people, we might surmise that they primarily value money, fame, and power and that they are perhaps a bit arrogant in their desire to reveal their influence to people.

In addition to a person's general presentation and environment, also consider your own visceral reactions to the person and calibrate your judgments accordingly. When we're around others, we have reflexive physiological and emotional reactions. Perhaps we feel instantly anxious—we break out into a cold sweat and our heart pounds. Perhaps we feel threatened and tense up. Perhaps we feel soothed or relaxed in the other person's presence—our blood pressure decreases and our muscles relax. Perhaps we feel drawn to another person, as if they exert a magnetic pull on us.

The ability to watch ourselves and become aware of what we're physically feeling at any given moment is what psychologists call *interoception*, and we can utilize it to fine-tune our interpretation of others' personalities. When I am deep in conversation with someone, I will sometimes ask myself: "How am I feeling right now? How am I physically experiencing this person right now?" We all have this built-in "spidey sense," but many of us don't actively pay attention to it. I was reminded of this phenomenon recently when watching *American Idol*. Every so often when one of the judges, Luke Bryan, hears someone really good, he'll look at fellow judge Katy Perry, hold up his arm for her to see, and say, "Look. Chill bumps."

What he's talking about is a physiological reaction he gets when he hears someone singing in such a way that affects him. I grew up calling them "goose bumps," but the point is the same: Bryan is attentive to those moments when his body is telling him something about the person with whom he's interacting. This is interoception, and we should all pay more attention to these signals when making judgments about people.

A fourth source of data we can use to calibrate our judgments is information about our own biases. All of us harbor biases about others—an inclination to prejudge them, to rely on stereotypes. Further, nearly all of us unfortunately fall prey to implicit or unconscious bias, no matter how much we hate to admit it. This is the nature of systemic racism and discrimination of all types. In their book, *Blindspot: Hidden Biases of Good People*, the scholars Mahzarin R. Banaji and Anthony G. Greenwald highlight the unconscious beliefs we hold and how they affect our assessment of others.[7] The authors describe their experience with the Implicit Association Test (IAT), which uncovers such beliefs. If you have not taken the IAT before (it's available free in an archived site at https://implicit .harvard.edu/implicit/), I urge you to take a few moments and see how your own biases affect your judgment—you will be surprised. The truth is that we all have implicit biases against people who are not like us, and we can make terrible errors in judgment when those biases go unchecked.

The key to preventing these errors is *awareness* of our biases and how they may be affecting our ability to read people. To judge others effectively, we must enter conversations with clarity about the sociocultural biases we might have, including those related to gender, race, religion, and class, and how they skew our judgment. This point about biases cannot be overstated: biases serve us (and society more broadly) poorly and do real harm. We should always check ourselves when making judgments about others, asking what personal biases are factoring into our assessment.

We also harbor a range of cognitive biases that we must recognize lest they warp our judgments of others. Some of these biases are well known and well documented. Confirmation bias (arguably the most important one) causes us to give more credence to information about personality that confirms what we already think. Similarity bias causes us to regard more positively the personalities of people who seem similar to us. Availability bias causes us to favor beliefs supported by evidence that is readily at hand (for instance, we might rush to regard someone as intelligent because they happened to say something smart and it really stuck in our minds).

Several other, lesser-known biases also crop up when we glean personality traits (the identification of such biases has become somewhat of a sport among research psychologists). The "hot hand fallacy" leads us to regard someone's success as more likely if they've already experienced a previous success (we might quickly conclude that someone possesses the traits of a strong leader if we learn that they led a platoon in the army). Perhaps more peculiar was the finding by Israeli researcher Shai Danziger and his colleagues that parole board judges tend to be more severe before a lunch break than after lunch. They called it the "hungry judge effect" (I think the "hangry effect" would have been a much better moniker!) and extrapolated that our assessments of others are affected by our satiety (this finding has come under some scrutiny over the last few years, but it is interesting nonetheless).[8] Clearly, physiological states like being under the influence of drugs or alcohol, being tired or stressed, and being pressed for time all affect our decisions, and we need to be aware of it.

As our conversations proceed and our hypotheses about others become firmer, we should question how our biases might be skewing our judgment and adjust our thinking accordingly. In some cases, delaying or avoiding decision-making until we can be freer from bias is the right course of action. In other cases, it's important to seek out additional data about people to test our perspectives.

A final way to calibrate and fine-tune our judgments is simply to tell the people whom we're judging what we're noticing and gauge their reactions. Doing this can build rapport, since it shows people that we really are listening to what they're saying. But it can also lead to important insights and prevent you from misjudging others. When I'm trying to suss out someone's personality, I might say something like "You know, you said that details are very important to you, and I noticed that you also gave a very detailed account of your work over the years. You told me how meticulous you were about your schoolwork as a kid and how spotless your dorm room was in college. And you're dressed very neatly today and arrived right on time. I'm getting the sense that you like everything just so—that you might have a perfectionist streak. Does that resonate with you?"

If the person agrees with your assessment, that might serve to validate your impressions of them, leaving you even more sure of your judgment. If they disagree, then an opportunity exists to gather more information. If they object vehemently, perhaps they really are a perfectionist but have difficulty seeing or accepting it. That would alert you to a lower level of self-awareness. In disagreeing, they might offer different explanations for the behavior you've noticed. Maybe they're only meticulous in certain situations or contexts. In academic or professional contexts, they're detail-oriented but in their private life they tend to take a more laid-back approach. Such an explanation, if it conforms with other data you've gathered, gives you a more nuanced sense of their perfectionist tendencies and helps you fill the Diligence box.

BE CURIOUS

YOU CAN MOBILIZE NEARLY any conversation to gather information about a person's character. The five strategies described in this chapter—build rapport, get people to talk about their past, ask power questions, interpret data, and calibrate the interpretation—aren't especially complex, but they do require practice to do well and get right. Ultimately, each of these strategies requires one thing: deep curiosity. You have to be interested in people and what makes them tick. Just as journalists conducting interviews seek to dig beneath the surface and uncover what's really going on in a given story, you need to try to pierce the personas that all of us construct in social situations in order to get to the essence of other people. Strive to muster the journalist's critical and synthetic eye and capacity to weave disparate pieces of information into a coherent story. Using the Personality Blueprint as your guide, ask follow-up questions, compare pieces of evidence with one another, and test your hypotheses by cultivating a range of other data.

Distractions abound in modern life, especially the addictive allure of our omnipresent smartphones. But if you can learn to lift your head up both literally and figuratively, lean into casual conversations throughout your day, and be curious about others and how they tick, you can enjoy a powerful advantage in business and in life.

KEY INSIGHTS

- Although personality is readily visible in what people say and do, we often must do a bit of work to glean specific traits people have.
- Casual conversations provide a great opportunity for

amassing data about others' personalities, if you know how to conduct them.

- Five strategies can help you to enhance your perceptivity during casual conversations: build rapport, get people to talk about their past, ask power questions, interpret data, and calibrate the interpretation.

- Deploying these five strategies leads us to approach conversations much like a journalist does when interviewing sources. It's important not merely to listen closely but to think critically and synthetically.

- Conversation is very much a lost art today, given the profusion of communications technology. We have so much to gain by rethinking how we interact socially, with an eye toward developing and exercising our perceptivity.

Chapter 4

THE RIGHT STUFF

BILL AND CAROL MURPHY, two professionals living in New England, were out to dinner with another young couple, Mark and Roseanne Gorman, when they began talking about possible new business ventures. The Murphys had been thinking of buying an investment property by the beach, and it turned out that the Gormans had a similar interest. As the waiter opened a second bottle of wine, Mark had an intriguing thought: What if the two couples went in on a property together and created a small business renting it out? It sounded like a wonderful opportunity. Bill and Mark were both good with their hands and interested in buying a fixer-upper that they could renovate. The two couples both had small children, which made for similar constraints on their time and budgets. By going in together, the couples could minimize the expense and the work involved.

Although Bill didn't know the Gormans well, he felt pretty comfortable going into business with them. Carol worked closely with Roseanne and could attest that she was extremely smart, conscientious, levelheaded, and affable. Mark seemed to be a great guy as well. At dinner, he came across as polite, interesting, and easy to get along with, if a bit quiet. Bill looked forward to getting to know him better and hopefully to building a nice little business together.

Within a few months, the couples found a property right on the beach with great potential and at an attractive price. The place needed extensive renovations throughout, but it was nothing that Bill and Mark couldn't handle. The two couples quickly drew up an agreement between themselves, arranged for a mortgage, closed on the property, and began the renovations. To push them along, the two men hired a couple of day laborers to help them.

It wasn't long, however, before tensions arose. As Bill discovered, Mark had a tendency to take on projects without thinking through how he would complete them. He then became overwhelmed and wound up accomplishing very little—a classic "overpromise, underdeliver" problem. Mark's reserved nature also seemed to pose an issue. If something bothered him or if a situation arose, he wouldn't communicate his misgivings at first, preferring to behave as if everything was fine. The tension would build up inside him, leading to an explosion of anger directed both at Bill and the tradespeople they were employing.

This dynamic as well as the inability to execute on projects led to ongoing drama between Bill and Mark. Because of poor planning, the project ran over budget and was behind schedule. Although Bill and Mark managed to maintain a workable relationship between them, the whole experience was much more stressful than Bill had anticipated, leaving him reluctant to ever take on a partner again.

When investing in a business, agreeing to go to work for a boss, forging a romantic partnership, or hiring someone for an important job, it's vitally important to understand how others tick. Unfortunately, many companies and individuals either pay only cursory attention to personality or describe character in ways that are ill-considered or unhelpful. Hiring managers write job postings with no clear sense of the traits that would allow someone to succeed in a given position and business context. An entrepreneur hiring a general manager for a fast-growing, socially responsive tech start-up, for instance, might say in an online job posting that they're looking for someone who is results-oriented, given to working long hours, and data-driven. But won't everyone interested in the job make such claims about themselves?

These qualities matter, of course, but they're superficial—they don't amount to a thoughtful description of the kind of person who would thrive in the job, and they certainly aren't easy to spot. If the entrepreneur really delved into it, they might find they need a general manager who is a self-starter, open-minded to new ideas and not stuck in their ways, adaptive to change and uncertainty, capable of communicating across differences, purpose-driven and oriented toward community, and passionate in their efforts to communicate and sell ideas, to name just a few. Notice how much more nuanced this picture of the desired general manager is compared with the generic attributes found in typical job descriptions.

Companies and individuals that do consider personality with more sophistication have difficulty screening for it, often relying on gut feelings or popular tests that are unscientific and worthless. You might have taken the Myers-Briggs test at some point in your career, including when applying for a job. Guess what? There is *zero* science behind it.[1] An employer would do just as well to assess someone's horoscope or the bumps on their head when making its selection. Likewise, you might have gone on a dating website like eHarmony to find your soul mate, filling out a personality questionnaire so that the algorithm could match you with people whose personalities are compatible with yours. As research has suggested, you would get results that are just as good if you pulled a name randomly out of a hat.[2]

Early in my career, I joined a boutique HR consultancy that specialized in "outplacement"—that is, helping people at client companies who had been laid off find their next gig. It wasn't especially glamorous work, but it often had a huge impact on individual employees who were desperately searching for jobs. As I came on board, my bosses introduced me to a tool called Forté they were using to assess candidates for jobs. Candidates received a short list of word pairs and were supposed to circle the element of each pair that they liked best. Based on these choices, Forté yielded some complex and nuanced information about their personality characteristics. But there was no way, I thought, that a test could determine so much from just a few circled words. When I looked into it, I found that the test was indeed unreliable and invalid—as worthless as Myers-Briggs.

I tried gently educating my bosses, but while I want to believe they meant well, they didn't want to hear it. Someone had sold them a seemingly cheap, efficient solution that they could market to their clients, so they wanted to believe in that solution's value. When they asked me to use this tool to help assess candidates for jobs, I was horrified. I would be making consequential decisions that would impact real people using a tool with no scientific basis. I just couldn't do it, and not long after I left the firm.

Such quackery is endemic in the psychological testing field. Untold numbers of important decisions are made every year based on tests that are essentially pseudoscience, leading to real suffering in the form of on-the-job failure, bankrupt businesses, early divorces, and more. Imagine if you lost out on a job or promotion because your scores on an unscientific test didn't yield the right results. Maybe the tests said you were confrontational and overly competitive when in fact you were nothing of the sort. How would you feel? Unscientific tests are not only unfair; they also tarnish the good scientific tests out there, and in some cases cause real, lasting harm.

Personal interviews as commonly conducted also offer little help when hiring people. Many bosses (and people on the dating scene!) spend more time during formal interviews talking than listening. In unstructured interviews, they ask generic, subjective questions (for instance, "What are your strengths and weaknesses?" or "Where do you see yourself in five years?") that don't elicit much—if any—reliable information about character. In the absence of data and a methodical way of analyzing it, many people wind up "listening to their gut" when judging others, arriving at decisions that are frequently incorrect because they rely on rampant stereotypes, biases, and prejudices discussed in the previous chapter.

Our cognitive biases during interviews also frequently hamper us when selecting others. We might look more favorably on candidates interviewed more recently (recency bias) or that we find more physically attractive (attractiveness bias). We might presume that a candidate with an impressive accomplishment on their résumé—a Harvard degree or a Fulbright scholarship—is exceptionally talented simply because they survived the selection process (survivorship bias). We might judge candidates more favorably who look like us or have elements of their background in common with us (similarity bias). Most people unwittingly fall prey to the halo effect when judging others: We see one positive characteristic about someone and automatically assume that they possess other positive characteristics, too. A physically attractive candidate, we presume, must also be a good communicator, a persuasive salesperson, and affable around others. A smart person must be levelheaded, prudent, and emotionally mature. Nonsense—these attributes are mutually exclusive, and we shouldn't assume that they are connected in any way.

There is a scientific basis for effectively selecting people using the Personality Blueprint described in Chapter 2. It is the way I help my clients understand their leadership candidates and choose whom to hire. It will enable you to pick the right people who have the dispo-sition and capability to do what the role requires. I should talk for a moment about the concept of "fit." Over the past few years, we've seen some backlash around hiring for culture fit.[3] The argument is that by hiring for fit, you hire for sameness. If you only hire people who fit into your culture, you exclude people who don't look and act like everyone else in the company. Of course, that leads to culture stagnation at best and discrimination at worst. I agree. I don't think you should ever hire purely for culture fit. When I assess people for selection, I am focused on who has the capability to execute the role effectively. That often includes the ability to mesh with others in the company, and also often includes the ability to add to the culture. The whole idea is whether a person will be able to do what needs to be done in the specific role and in the specific environment. That should be your objective in assessing anyone for selection, too.

PEOPLE ARE MORE THAN SCORES ON A TEST

BEFORE DETAILING HOW TO use my assessment method, let me say a bit more about formal personality testing. An extensive body of research demonstrates that some personality tests *are* scientif-ically valid and useful in determining core aspects of personality, predicting some behaviors and attitudes on the job.[4] My colleagues and I use these tests as one component of our robust selection as-sessments. For example, we use a popular test called the Hogan Per-sonality Inventory to understand core personality traits and how they show up in the workplace (more on the Hogan tests later in the book). However, as I suggested earlier, a good psychometric test extracts basic traits, but not how they are expressed. This severely limits our ability to make good judgments about a person's fit for a role. To do that properly, you need a deeper level of understanding about the person. You need to understand who they really are.

Recruiting firms know clients want to hear something about personality, so many of them will administer a test to say that they've used one. But people are much more than scores on a test or the credentials or experiences on their résumés. They are complex, and we gain nothing by reducing them to a number or where they went to college. Psychometrically sound personality tests combined with the personality-based interviewing techniques presented in this book is the winning formula for making good hiring decisions.

THE IMPORTANCE OF CONTEXT

EVERY SELECTION PROCESS BEGINS with context. Before trying to assess someone's personality, you must clarify what you're assessing them for. Every business environment is unique, with a different culture, operating environment, strategy, set of leaders, and so on. Only by assessing a given context will we be in a position to judge whether someone can fit into a given role. Let's say I assess a shy person for a retail sales role. That shyness might negatively affect this person's ability to succeed in the role and is therefore highly relevant. However, if I assess that same person for a government accounting job, his shyness might not be as relevant as it will be more consistent with the environment. Same person, different context.

So many people neglect to begin with the outcomes in mind when hiring. Too often, companies cobble together some half-baked job description they likely found online or have used numerous times in other situations. Most major recruiting firms have benchmarks for what people in certain roles *should* have in terms of disposition. They market their benchmarks of thousands of CFOs, CHROs, or other executives, letting prospective clients think they will get a sense of how their candidate stacks up against peers in that position.

Such benchmarks may seem helpful with respect to required experiences, but they are much less so in terms of dispositional requirements. Because companies vary depending on their industry, geography, historical context, products, competitive challenges, long-term objectives, strategies, and more, the precise bundle of personality traits that would help their leaders succeed will vary. A person who is sharp, analytic, creative, open-minded, adaptive, growth-oriented, and entrepreneurial might thrive as the leader of a fast-growth start-up. But if this same person were to take a job at a large, global corporation, they might not fare as well. In that context, success might mean having a personality well suited to running a sprawling bureaucracy and operating within a well-established global culture—in other words, being more operationally focused, systems-oriented, diligent, capable of communicating to a wide array of audiences and across cultures, and so on.

One study of 9,000 leaders across dozens of global firms identified some 300 contextual challenges confronting leaders, everything from strategic objectives like the need to grow market share to organizational ones like the need to reform an unhealthy culture. As researchers found, the suitability of a leader's personality, experience, and skills to the specific tasks before them was the most important factor determining their success. Comparing leaders to horses, one researcher noted, "Companies have been hiring and developing these generic workhorse leaders when what they really need is a thoroughbred whose strengths are specifically suited to a particular racetrack."[5]

CREATE A SUCCESS PROFILE

RATHER THAN MAKING A list of the traits you think you'll need in the person you hire, create an actual Success Profile, taking it as the criteria against which you will evaluate prospective candidates. Ask yourself: Who do we *really* want? This starts with a focus on outcomes. What does the person need to accomplish? What will they need to actually do in order to be successful? The trick here is to ask these questions multiple times, probing to more fundamental levels of analysis. Most of us are too hasty in defining success. We know the obvious outcomes we seek, but we don't ponder the many underlying behaviors and abilities that define success in even relatively low-level roles.

At my firm, one of our executive assistants got engaged and moved with her fiancé to New Zealand. So, we had to recruit for a new assistant. We started by pulling together an obvious list of job duties. We wanted our new assistant to be organized, able to multitask, able to handle a busy consultant's schedule, and so on. But then we asked ourselves: What does this person *really* need to accomplish in order for us to judge them a success? Well, they have to be able to reduce the anxiety of the consultant with whom they're working. They have to be able to interact well with different personalities in our office. They have to be able to keep everyone safe and on schedule when coordinating business travel. They have to interact well with our clients, strengthening their trust in our firm and our brand. Ultimately, they have to help our team deliver so that our clients ultimately feel secure in their people decisions. With this deeper understanding of the job in mind, we were better positioned to pick the right new assistant for us.

Be sure as well to think about the broader cultural context in which the person you select will operate. What values and related behaviors define your organizational or team culture? Focus here not on the corporate mission or vision statement conveyed on the company's website, but on the culture to which you aspire. Think about your culture as it actually is. Who really makes it in your company? And who utterly fails to fit in? Consider personality-related problems you might have encountered in the past and that you don't wish to repeat going forward. Think, too, about qualities that the best people in your company almost always have. Are they collaborative? Able to empathize with customers? Strong, willful decision-makers? Highly competitive? Ethical? Something else?

Think, too, about your values. Alignment around values plays a vital role in determining whether someone will be a good fit for you and your company, so it should be a part of your Success Profile. When considering corporate values as they apply to the Success Profile, move beyond what's written on the framed graphic hanging on your boardroom wall. (Integrity is on the list, I'm sure, but what does that mean?) Think about the values that most represent your company. What beliefs and principles guide behavior? How do you define right and wrong? How do you treat employees and customers in a way that reflects what matters to you most?

We've so far focused on what is true for us and our organizations *now* when thinking about the broader context. You should also contemplate the future and what you hope to achieve. I ask our clients to consider their company's strategy when forming the Success Profile. What will their business look like in three, five, or ten years? How will the company get there, and what will it need to do in the interim to execute on those strategies? What traits will a leader or partner need in order to help execute the strategy?

If your company's goal is to expand into new geographies over the next five to ten years, it might require leaders who can engage in big-picture thinking, have a global mindset, are collaborative and able to forge alliances with a range of partners, are open to new cultures and experiences, and so forth. Similarly, if your company has roots as a start-up but is rapidly scaling up, you'll probably want a leader with the temperament required to manage more sophisticated systems and establish formal processes and procedures. If your goals involve an IPO down the road, it will be important for key leaders to be credible to Wall Street, financially savvy, and comfortable in a more regulated environment.

In pondering future goals and strategies, think especially about any specific external challenges you or your organization will need to surmount and how that might translate into personality traits necessary for success. Is your market becoming more competitive? You're going to need people who are hard-driving, "elbows out," and ready for battle. Has a disruptive technology appeared on the horizon that will affect your future operating environment? Add adaptability, tech-savvy, and future-focused to your list of required traits. (We currently see employers doing precisely this. As of this writing, the financial services sector is undergoing significant disruption. As a result, digital fluency, flexibility, and unconventional thinking now are price-of-admission traits for successful job candidates, even at traditional banks.)

The recent history of the tech giant Microsoft illustrates the perils of not anticipating future challenges when selecting leaders as well as the benefits that accrue when we do. During the 2000s, online search became a major business, mobile telephony proliferated across the globe, and social media snared millions of users. To take advantage of these trends, Microsoft needed a visionary leader capable of taking risks and inspiring the organization to grow and change. Steve Ballmer, who succeeded founding CEO Bill Gates as the company's chief executive, was not that leader. Rather than a tech geek, he was a more conventional finance guy and deal-maker.

Under his leadership, the company became mired in bureaucracy and politics and stuck to formidable yet conventional products like Windows, Office, and enterprise servers, missing a wealth of opportunity and prompting some to regard his tenure as Microsoft's "lost decade." As one journalist put it, the company "became a high-tech equivalent of a Detroit car-maker, bringing flashier models of the same old thing off of the assembly line even as its competitors upended the world."[6]

In 2014, after Ballmer abruptly announced that he would step down as CEO, the company appointed as his replacement Satya Nadella, a leader who by virtue of his temperament was well suited to help the company face its future challenges. Microsoft at the time needed a reboot. It had to learn once more how to be nimble, customer-focused, visionary, collaborative, and agile so that it could compete in what would likely be an era of rapid and ongoing disruption. As a leader, Nadella proved himself to be empathetic, innovative, and humble—the kind of person who could inspire an organization to change. One of his first priorities was to lead a renaissance of Microsoft's culture, emphasizing learning and development.

Nadella was also a tech visionary capable of anticipating shifts in markets. He partnered with previous competitors like Apple, Salesforce, and Dropbox, and spearheaded brilliant acquisitions like Mojang (the gaming company that makes *Minecraft*) and the social media network LinkedIn. More recently, it seems that Nadella made an incredibly shrewd early investment in OpenAI, the company that makes ChatGPT. His success and Ballmer's less successful track record should remind us:

When choosing leaders, we need to focus not just on what we need now, but on what we *will* need in the future.

To build your Success Profile, write down the relevant context that the new leader will face. Then, using the Personality Blueprint introduced in the last chapter, translate the context into required personal attributes. Take your time—you really want an exhaustive set of personality criteria against which to evaluate candidates for the role. Once you have a long list of traits, organize them into a manageable set of categories. Try to arrive at four to five big-picture areas against which to evaluate candidates, with longer lists of sub-traits attached to each.

Figure 4 provides two sample Success Profiles, showing how categories broke down for two of my clients ("Company #1" and "Company #2") that were evaluating candidates for senior leadership positions. These are abridged versions; in the actual Profiles, we included more traits under each category—about ten to twelve. Although these two Success Profiles overlap to some extent, reviewing them side by side confirms how differing contexts can lead to different blueprints.

COMPANY #1

Category #1: Problem Solving
Outstanding intellectual ability and judgment.
High attention to accuracy and quality.
Good to great commercial judgment.
Analytical rigor; able to diagnose potential areas of risk and
  opportunity.
Patient and forward-thinking. Have the firm's long-term
  interest constantly in mind.

Category #2: Productivity

Hardworking and internally motivated. Thrive off the work.

Strong attention to detail and tactical excellence.

High standards for excellence but not paralyzed by perfection.

Structured and disciplined without being rigid.

Category #3: Interpersonal Impact

Have an unwavering focus on relationships.

Establish rapport easily.

Gain and maintain trusted access and become a confidant to executives at partner companies.

Socially versatile, can work with all levels in a company.

Seek input from collaborators in the company.

Category #4: Adaptability/Growth

Optimism. See the upside and focus on solutions rather than just problems.

Very self-aware; know strengths and limitations. Open to getting support from others, if needed (deal team, outside expertise).

Aware of how one impacts others in multiple settings.

Show independence of thought.

Actively work on own development needs and potential derailers.

Resilient. Come up with new solutions when faced with setbacks.

Category #5: Traits Relevant to the Company Culture

Nonhierarchical. Able to get things done rather than focus on politics and ambition.

Demanding but supportive. Push for the highest quality work while always respecting others.

Have a level of sophistication without seeming above others.

Possess a "we're in this together" mindset. Do good work for the firm, not for oneself.

Collaborative. Openly share and learn from others. Solve problems together.

Be respectful and considerate of others. Care about colleagues.

Manage stress productively. Cope well with stress and workloads.

COMPANY #2

Category #1: Big Thinking

Business acumen—know the business, industry, or market influences (for example, impact of market trends, political/regulatory events, disruptions, customer demands).

Prioritize innovation—seek new ways of doing things in order to be more efficient or productive. Leverage technology to do so.

Financial acumen—understand the industry, how to become profitable, and how to quantify outcomes.

Forward thinking—anticipate the downstream effects of decisions.

Parallel thinking—possess strategic capabilities and execution "know how."

Smart—capacity to handle high volume and complexity of information.

Category #2: Productivity

Strong work ethic—gets it done until results can be seen.

Goal-driven—not easily sidetracked or intimidated despite environment of high ambiguity.

Bias for action—observe but then quickly move to action.

Sense of urgency—move fast, create fast, reprioritize as needed.

Strive for flawless execution; care about the details and quality of one's own work. Undaunted by high expectations.

Flexible scope management—can switch from strategic to tactical or operational detail orientation.

Category #3: Interpersonal Fortitude

Have thick skin and don't take feedback personally

Honest and transparent—maintain an appropriate flow of communication, no hidden agenda.

Balance listening with influencing.

Flexible communication. Influence a wide range of stakeholders, including professionals, employees, investors, corporate colleagues, etc.

Composed in a crisis—show emotional intelligence and restraint; read between the lines; have insight into self, others, and facts of situation; adjust behavior.

Have the courage to take a stand in unpopular settings but in a way that creates better outcomes rather than conflict.

Category #4: People Leadership

Motivator—find ways to rally team members; convey ways to be aggressive with opportunity but not with people.

Change manager—support and acclimatize team through new practices. See change as a process.

Set high bar for performance—want fast results and high quality.

Unblock obstacles—help others deal with setbacks (versus sink-or-swim mentality); advocate on their behalf; problem-solve with team.

On the ball—follow up and monitor progress, to know what's going on.

Hold self and others accountable for timely and high-quality results.

Category #5: Values

High energy, drive, and grit.

Sense of personal ownership and accountability in all matters.

Entrepreneurial—embrace speed, change, uncertainty and keep up with new ideas (maintain the "start-up culture").

Question the status quo—competitive, driven, ask "can it be done better?"

High sense of personal responsibility and integrity—believe in being the architect of one's own actions and success.

Self-aware. Know strengths and limitations as a leader.

Figure 4: Success Profile for an Executive Search Decision

THE DEEP-DIVE INTERVIEW

WITH THE PROFILE IN mind, it's time to get as much personality data from your candidate as possible. I'll share with you now the way I conduct what I call deep-dive interviews. This is how I get the data I need to advise my clients on critical hiring decisions. If you want to make better judgments about people, follow this process as closely as you can.

A good deep-dive interview requires time. It can't be rushed. When I am assessing a candidate for a role, we set aside three hours for the in-depth interview. In some everyday situations, that isn't possible. What is nonnegotiable, though, is holding the interview in a private setting, free from distractions or prying eyes. Meet in a comfortable room and ensure you have a direct, eye-to-eye sight line with the person you are interviewing.

Put away your list of questions, including those behavior-based questions you were told would help you. These are the kind of questions you've seen in interview guides or been on the receiving end of yourself: "Describe a time when you showed leadership in the face or ambiguity. What was the situation, what did you do, and what was the outcome?" While it may seem counterintuitive to some, it is my professional experience in assessing thousands of people over twenty years that behavior-event questions seem rigid and rote, and you won't actually glean anything about the person in front of you by relying on them.

Before beginning your interview, have a pen and notebook in front of you. Organize the page into boxes, each corresponding to a box from the Personality Blueprint. I draw a line down the middle of the page (making two columns), then draw two horizontal lines, creating six boxes. I devote one of these boxes to each of the five Blueprint boxes and the sixth to gathering insights about the person's self insight and other relevant data. I write Intellect in the top left, Emotionality in the top right, Sociability in the middle left, Drive in the middle right, and Diligence in the bottom left. I leave the bottom right blank. With this structure before you, you're ready to start interviewing the person and filling in the boxes as the conversation proceeds.

I discussed some of the techniques you'll want to use during the interview in the previous chapter, but I'll recall them here for you to help you see how they fit together. Start by building rapport. It's very important that the person feels relaxed and not like they are being interrogated. Developing chemistry, getting them laughing, and dialing down the intensity sets the stage for a much more open and revealing conversation. Another way to get people comfortable is to speak candidly about the meeting's purpose. Lacking information, people can assume the worst.

I tell people that my hope is to understand them better. I go on to explain that who we are as people is, in part, a function of our experiences, so I am interested in hearing about theirs. I explain that I'm a very curious person, so I will be asking all kinds of questions about their personal and work history to get to know them better. I tell them that the conversation is strictly confidential, and that I will be taking the insights I glean, synthesizing them with the results of any personality tests I may have had them complete, and arriving at some conclusions about how well they fit the role for which they are being considered. Finally, I explain that no matter what the final decision is, I will be happy to go over my findings with them, giving them any feedback I have.

I carefully word this preamble to provide informed consent and allay any previous concerns the interviewee may have had. I know the kinds of concerns people have going into an interview like this, and I do my best to put people at ease.

I then proceed to ask the interviewee about their current working life. The idea here is simply to get them talking. People are naturally guarded when you first meet them, especially when they know you are evaluating them. You must break the ice somehow, without doing all the talking. Get them to tell you anything, really. I begin this phase of the interview assessment by asking the person some easy and relatively superficial questions about their present circumstances. Can they describe their current role to me? What do they do and what is the reporting structure? How long have they worked there? What are they most proud of? If I asked the person's boss to describe them, what would the boss say? These basic questions elicit all kinds of benign responses. That's the point: I am not interrogating, but rather encouraging—and getting—the person to talk.

Importantly, speak directly to the person and pay very close attention to them. You have your notebook handy and are categorizing important insights, but put away your laptop; it creates a physical barrier between you and the person you are trying to assess. You can't really see the person and pick up on nuance if you're tapping away at a keyboard and your eyes are glued to the screen. Watch and listen to the person and what they are really telling you.

Once you've gotten them talking, it's time to start getting a read on their personalities. As I've suggested, we are, in many ways, a function of our histories: the decisions we made, the people with whom we surrounded ourselves, the lessons we learned, the challenges we overcame. To truly understand a person, you must uncover the essence of their journey. So, get them talking about their past. The best way to do that is to help them organize their story chronologically.

To learn about their early life, ask them to describe how their parents inspired or influenced them. How does their own disposition compare with that of their parents? As discussed in Chapter 3, this is such a revealing question. Most people don't expect it, especially in an interview scenario, and they don't immediately know how to answer. They say things like "My father was not really a risk-taker, whereas I am much more ambitious and willing to go outside my comfort zone"; or "My mother was very nurturing and an emotional person, and I get that from her." These are important insights. I go on to inquire about their siblings and the effect that their place in the birth order had on them.

As I ask about interviewees' early lives, I often gain access to important information about character. I will periodically hear about a person who grew up on a farm and had to get up every day at four in the morning to milk the cows. This person might have cultivated traits associated with Box #5, Diligence. Other times, I hear about someone whose family moved frequently during their childhood since their parent was in the military. This person might have found it difficult to retain relationships, forcing them to develop as an extrovert who can quickly connect with new friends.

When you feel you've learned enough about a person's early childhood, go on to high school. I often spend a great deal of time in the high school years, mostly because this is where most of us begin forming our identities. We change and mature throughout our lives, of course, but as teenagers we establish the basic ingredients of our personalities. Ask interviewees a range of questions, including: What were their favorite or strongest subjects? What was their social life like? What did they like to do with their friends? What sorts of people did they tend to form friendships with and what sort did they tend to avoid? Did they participate in sports, the arts, or some other hobby? Did they work any jobs during school? What were those experiences like? If we could wave a magic wand and see them back in high school, what would we see—what kind of person? How are they still like that person and how (beyond the obvious) have they changed? As they neared the end of high school, what were they thinking of doing next? How did they decide their next move? Who influenced them the most at that point in their life?

Next, go on to ask about college. Did your interviewee go to college, or did they choose another route? How did they make that decision? If they did go to college, how did they choose where to go? What was the transition to college like? Where did they live? Did they have a roommate? How successful was their first year? What kind of work and personal habits did they maintain? Did they tend to stay up late or get up early? Were they messy or neat? What kind of student were they: someone who did a little bit each day in order to prepare for an exam or a crammer? What classes appealed to them? How did they pick their major? What big revelations, if any, did they have during their college years? In what ways did they grow as a person? Did anything else memorable happen to them, positive or negative? Were they in a fraternity or sorority, and why?

At this point, I do a seemingly innocuous thing that actually has essential implications: I announce what I call "the Break." Taking a ten-minute break at around the halfway mark of any job interview is one of the most important structural techniques I can convey to you. Most interviewees think the Break is about halting the questioning. They think it is about what is not being said, the absence of material to process. In fact, there are important psychological processes that can be accessed only by the Break. It serves as a kind of reset on the conversation, giving me a chance to process what I know about the person and what I need to know. But more important than my own reflections is what is going on inside the interviewee's head. I know that they are ruminating on what has just transpired. I have asked them all sorts of questions about their history and personality, and they're quickly running through the answers they've given. They're wondering if they said anything too revealing or that otherwise would not get them the job in question. They're also processing my questions and how they likely surprised themselves in their answers. When we reconvene, we can both step outside the conversation a bit and reflect on it together. In my experience, interviewees tend to divulge more after they've had a chance to process what they've already said.

Many people use the technique of taking a break while dating, perhaps without realizing it. If you're out on a date, excuse yourself after a while to go the restroom. Use that time strategically. Think hard about what you know about the other person and what you still want to know. When you return, reset the conversation. If you don't do this already, you'll find that it takes the conversation to a whole new level.

In an employee interview, I follow our breaks with a question that solicits interviewees' impressions of the conversation thus far. Does anything particularly resonate with them or give them pause? They tend to say things like "I never really thought about how I am similar to my mother" or "It's really interesting what has changed since high school and what hasn't." Often they offer new information about stories they've told, revealing more about their personalities. I'll sometimes ask interviewees to reflect back on themselves as if from an outside vantage point: "In thinking about the first part of our conversation, and the story you have told about yourself, how would you characterize that person?" This question can elicit new insight and self-reflection that helps me to refine and validate my hypotheses. It prompts people to reveal some portion of the inner dialogue they have about themselves and their identities. Never forget to take the Break.

When we've jointly processed what they have been thinking about, I steer the interviewee back to their personal history. After finishing college, what were they thinking in terms of next steps? What was the transition into the working world like? Did they forge any helpful relationships with bosses or colleagues? What did they like or dislike most about their first job? What were their early performance reviews like? Where did they succeed, and where did they fail? What did they learn? What was their first experience like working under a manager? Looking back on it, what advice would they give to that manager? How or why did they decide to leave their first role? Ask similar questions about subsequent roles, probing into the relationships they built with bosses, colleagues, and others, and asking them to explain why they left and made any other career moves that they did.

Once your interviewee has taken their story back up to the present, ask them to think about the future and also their life outside of work. What are their career goals going forward? What do they think they need to work on professionally or personally so that they can achieve those goals? What is their family life like? If they have children, what parts of them show up in their kids or are expressed in their parenting? What else in life matters to them? What do they do for fun?

These are just some of the many questions I ask (also working in the power questions described in Chapter 3). The point isn't to be exhaustive about specific questions. It's simply to have a conversation with someone, allowing them enough opportunity to reveal their personalities. I allow myself a good deal of latitude to improvise in the moment, probing further into topics, experiences, or stories that would seem likely to yield the most data about character. I sometimes ask interviewees directly about themes I see emerging in their unfolding stories, and I also probe as much as I can into territory that seems to hold emotional value for them.

As mentioned in the last chapter, I'll sometimes make connections with my own life and experiences, as this helps to build rapport and encourage the interviewee to continue speaking freely. Although I stick to the general structure outlined here (present day followed by chronological narrative up to the present and beyond), it's important not to be too rigid. Again, if the interview seems rote or forced, interviewees will tense up and withhold information. Far better to help them feel like they're simply having a natural, friendly conversation about their lives with a stranger who is curious and engaged.

Try to make these interactions in person. Recruiting has largely moved online, but I think that's a mistake. So much is lost on video-conference and phone. Laggy Internet connections are the worst: it's impossible to pick up on nuances of verbal and nonverbal communication with choppy video or other latency effects. Even in the best of times, Internet bandwidth and videoconference technology lack the ability to transmit subtle changes in the outer bands of audio and video spectrums that we would otherwise detect in person. Meet the candidate in person if possible.

MOVE TOWARD A DECISION

THE INTERVIEW TECHNIQUES DESCRIBED here will have led you to develop deep insights about individuals and their character. After the interview concludes, allow time to reflect on the conversation and jot down more extensive notes. If you've been able to get the candidate to complete scientifically valid personality tests, go through the results of those and extract key insights about the person that also fit into the Blueprint. For example, the tests may indicate that a person is extroverted. If, thanks to your interview, you have insights around their gregarious, casual, and self-confident interpersonal style listed in the Sociability box of the Blueprint, you now have confirmation of the personality trait and how it is expressed specifically in this individual.

At this point, you have established the person's nuanced personality and core traits, and you've organized those traits coherently. The key to moving from good insights to good judgment lies in comparing the Blueprint with the Success Profile. How closely does this person fit the Profile? Are there categories in which they're particularly strong or weak? Think beyond personality as well. Does this person have the experience, knowledge, and skills they'll need to succeed in the role? How do they compare with other candidates you've interviewed, both in terms of the Success Profile and their other credentials?

Putting the Blueprint and Success Profile side by side, you should be able to discern whether the person fits the needs of the role. Your decision will be infinitely more informed than if you hadn't rigorously assessed personality, and your judgment will be better as a result. You can make the call with confidence.

I've focused on hiring decisions, but we can adapt this process to make selections in a host of professional and personal situations, whether it's choosing a dog-walker, deciding which heart specialist to go with, or deciding whether to start a new business venture with someone. One of the greatest benefits of this process is that it allows us to be much more thoughtful and deliberate. The process in this chapter turns us all into personality sleuths. Become more mindful of the kind of person you're seeking, and mobilize your curiosity about others to canvass for specific traits.

One area in which I hope we'll do more such sleuthing is in politics. People do take personality into account when making voting decisions, but they usually assess personality thoughtlessly and superficially. They quickly judge candidates based on political affiliations—the team they're on—and communication style, labeling one candidate as a "fighter," another as "low energy," yet another as "elitist." A certain ex-president was particularly good at magnifying negative personality traits of his rivals, labeling them in a schoolyard-bully-type way. While these labels may or may not accurately reflect the candidates' personalities, they give us a grossly incomplete reading, eliding the many dimensions and complexities of human character. These labels are also potentially irrelevant, as most of the time voters haven't begun to think in a systematic way about the personality traits that would allow the occupant of a given political office to succeed.

If you're a U.S. citizen reading this, you'll likely have to make important political decisions over the next few years. I urge you to use the insights contained in this book, your perceptivity in particular, to make good judgments. Start by constructing a Success Profile for the job. For example, what does the next president really need to accomplish during their term in office? What key stakeholders will they have to please, and how? What external challenges will they likely face, and what will it require to handle those successfully? Think hard about the specific personality traits and values that would help the next president to do an exceptional job as you define it, and just as important, which ones *wouldn't* help. Paint a detailed picture of the ideal candidate as objectively as you can without jumping ahead to assess actual candidates themselves.

Once you've created a clear Success Profile, start collecting data on the candidates. Scrutinize speeches, media interviews, books and other written materials authored by the candidates, and biographical information available online. If you're lucky enough, try to interact with candidates in person, even if only for a few minutes. The goal here is to try to glean real information about personality, as opposed to the public persona that candidates cultivate. Too often we rely on what we see in TV ads, tweets, or media spots to infer something about a candidate's personality. Having spent time with many public figures, including previous presidential candidates, I can assure you that what you see online or on television is usually nothing close to their true selves. Rather than relying on how the candidates' media teams have packaged their personalities, we must amass data ourselves and analyze it with our own methodology.

Using the Personality Blueprint, organize insights you can glean into the five category boxes. Continuously test those insights and assumptions as you obtain more data over time. In the end, you'll arrive at much better decisions about the candidates and vote accordingly. You'll have exercised good judgment.

GOING DEEP ON PEOPLE

ONE CLIENT OF MINE, a wealthy family that owned a well-known and very successful company in the aviation industry, faced the challenging task of selecting the company's next CEO. The current CEO, the family patriarch and a much-revered figure, was retiring after a successful thirty-year career, and the company's board sought to select the next CEO from among a dozen or so younger family members.

One candidate stood out among the rest: the CEO's son, Sam. Affable and intelligent, he had studied at elite colleges and done well. After a stint working at the family business, he had gone to medical school and spent a couple of years interning as a vascular surgeon. Then, his career had taken an unexpected turn. After tasting some locally made chocolate on a vacation and falling in love with its unique flavor, he came up with an idea for a new brand of organic chocolate products. Partnering with a famous rock musician, he launched the brand and devoted himself to building it up. His parents thought he was crazy to branch off as an entrepreneur—few family members had done so. But they didn't think he was so crazy over the next few years as the business grew, and they certainly didn't think he was crazy when he and his partner sold the business for $2 billion.

Although Sam had a number of other talented relatives with relevant experience who would have been good candidates for the CEO position, none had started a billion-dollar business. It wouldn't have been crazy for the board of the family company to call off its search and simply hand the CEO job to him. Even if they had considered other candidates, you might not have thought that the board would spend much time evaluating their personalities—these were family members, after all, and very well known to all involved. But that's exactly what this board did, hiring my colleagues and me to do the work. All told, we interviewed the board, creating a detailed Success Profile and conducting three-hour interviews with key candidates. We also had candidates take scientific personality tests.

The interviews turned up interesting findings, including some about Sam. We discovered that although he came across in a low-key way, he had a visionary's ability to anticipate future market conditions and was willing to take risks. He tended to be quite sociable and diplomatic in dealing with people, although at times he struggled to communicate clearly and directly. He was quite confident in his abilities and at the same time remained endearingly humble. He liked to feel stimulated, had a taste for adventure, liked to move quickly and decisively, and wasn't especially organized or interested in structures and systems. Many of these traits would prove helpful to him if he were to occupy the CEO's post, but I wondered whether he would find running a large, plodding company with an established business as fun and fulfilling as starting up an innovative company from scratch. If he didn't, he might flame out on the job, underperforming or leaving prematurely. In coming to its decision, the board would have to weigh these risks and also consider the strengths and weaknesses that other young family members might bring to the job.

As this board understood, it's important to spend the time to look beneath the surface and really understand people, even if you think you know them. Do you really understand what makes them tick, or are you acquainted only with isolated aspects of who they are? And how much have your own biases affected your judgments? You set yourself up for disaster when you don't take personality into account, but you also become vulnerable when you do consider it yet act on quick, unexamined impressions you might have of people.

The best approach is to take the time to study people and discern their underlying traits. You can do this on your own, without hiring a consultant like me. You can think of yourself as a student of behavior, a scientist, trying to understand this specimen in front of you. Pay close attention to what someone is saying, how they're saying it, and what it reveals about their core personality. Really seek to understand the other person. Probing into the personalities of candidates won't guarantee you'll make a great choice, but it sure does increase the odds.

KEY INSIGHTS

- When considering candidates for important roles in your professional or personal life, it's vitally important to understand how they tick.
- Formal tests can help us glean personality as part of a selection process, but be careful: Myers-Briggs and certain other popular personality tests are unscientific and worthless. The best approach is to use a scientifically rigorous test but rely primarily on qualitative personal interviews.
- To improve our perceptivity, we must improve how we conduct formal job interviews. The first step is to create a Success Profile that specifies exactly what traits are desirable given the role and its specific context.

- When conducting interviews, use the basic approach described in Chapter 2 but adapt it for the task at hand, making the conversation more extensive and structured.
- You can use this method at various stages of the selection process: when vetting a large, initial pool of candidates, when assessing your short list, and to validate your final choice once you've made it.

Chapter 5

SETTING RELATIONSHIPS
UP FOR SUCCESS

IN 2015, A PRIVATE equity (PE) firm I work with asked me to help them with "Platinum Jewelers," a high-growth jewelry retail business they were about to acquire. By all accounts, Platinum looked like a great bet. The company had an innovative business model, a winning strategy, and an experienced and talented executive team. And yet, the investment firm's partners did have one concern: although they had already decided to do the deal, they wondered how they might best manage a relationship with Danielle, Platinum's founder, whom they knew to be both brilliant and difficult. The firm was sinking a lot of capital into Platinum, and the partners anticipated having to work closely and harmoniously with Danielle to achieve the growth and profitability that everyone expected. The partners thought they would maximize their success if they understood Danielle better as a person, anticipated potential areas of conflict, knew how she needed to develop professionally in order to execute their investment thesis, and took steps to support her growth as a leader.

Born in the United Kingdom, Danielle had worked in finance herself before partnering with an experienced local jeweler and starting Platinum Jewelers. When I assessed her, I found that in many ways she had many of the attributes of the classic entrepreneur. She was intelligent and very shrewd, and like many entrepreneurs had "street smarts" rather than "book smarts"—she was highly intuitive, strategic, and practical-minded. She also was hardworking and extremely ambitious—she wanted to be a billionaire and didn't hesitate to let other people know it. She loved the freedom she had enjoyed to operate independently and was confident in her ability to spot opportunities and threats that others didn't see. She was a risk-taker—scrappy, aggressive, opportunistic, and happy to make a big bet impulsively. She loved the adrenaline rush of closing a big deal. Her default approach was to take risks based on gut feeling, without much concern for what had or hadn't worked in the past.

Danielle was quite sociable although not necessarily easy to be with. Her motto was "Work hard, play hard"—and boy did she like to party. She also liked to flaunt her power and wealth, to the point where she sometimes came across to others as inauthentic. She wasn't the most empathetic or sensitive boss out there. She got bored easily and would cut people off in conversation and move on when she lost interest. She didn't devote the time and careful communication required to obtain buy-in from her team when making big decisions. She was blunt and to the point, sometimes painfully so. If people around her didn't "get" what she was saying, too bad. She was so bright and quick that she sometimes didn't communicate her ideas clearly, nor did she take the time to think her ideas through before blurting them out. All told, others often perceived her as abrasive and a bit of a salesperson—not necessarily someone they could trust. On the other hand, Danielle was self-aware and understood how she sometimes rubbed people the wrong way, even if she didn't always take action to moderate her more counterproductive tendencies.

Assessing Danielle's personality, I saw three primary issues that she and my clients would need to manage in order to make the most of their investment. First, as they and Danielle grew Platinum together, she would have to hire or promote other seasoned executives and delegate responsibility to them. She couldn't run a massive business herself. Somehow, my clients would need to help her keep her taste for independence in check. Second, Platinum's new ownership structure would mean less room for impulsive risk-taking on Danielle's part. She would still have opportunities to take bold action, but she would also have to learn to make balanced, well-considered decisions in collaboration with her private equity partners, since she was playing with their money. Finally, I believed that Danielle's interpersonal intensity would rub people wrong in her growing business. To wield more influence as a boss, she'd have to tone down her flashy behavior and find ways to connect with a diverse group of stakeholders.

Knowing my PE firm clients as I did, I realized that Danielle's personality wasn't the only potential problem to watch. "Joe," one of the firm's senior partners, seemed particularly poised to clash with Danielle. An engineer by training, Joe was just as smart as Danielle, but whereas she was intuitive and conceptual—a true ideas person—Joe was much more linear, logical, and analytic. Joe also was conservative and buttoned up—quite a contrast to Danielle's vivacious, party-hard style. Joe was just as confident as Danielle and like her often came across as imposing and arrogant. Whereas Danielle could react impatiently when she became bored, Joe could belittle you or make you feel stupid if he disagreed with you. Given how forceful both Joe's and Danielle's personalities were, and how little finesse each of them sometimes showed when dealing with others, I worried that the two would struggle to forge a strong relationship built around trust and mutual respect. I also wondered how Danielle's ambition would square with Joe's establishment mindset. He was looking to protect his wealth, while she was looking to generate hers. How would they negotiate her taste for risk-taking, given that they were placing bets with Joe's money?

Most of us don't think very carefully about the nuances and practical implications of character—both others' and our own—either at the outset of work or personal relationships or later as we try to manage them. We don't anticipate potential pitfalls we might face given our own and others' characters, nor do we take preventative action. To improve our relationships, we think about post hoc strategies. That is, we wait until we are in a relationship and then look for things we can do in order to make them pleasant and productive. Conventional wisdom on how to optimize relationships focuses on areas like communicating clearly and honestly, demonstrating trustworthiness, respecting boundaries, working collaboratively, acknowledging others' strengths, soliciting feedback, staying open to new ideas, and showing empathy.[1]

Such common practices are great for managing relationships with people in general, but they're really just basic. Proactive strategies involving personality psychology are infinitely more powerful. One such strategy I deploy when a work relationship is about to begin is to develop a "user's manual" for people. Just as a user's manual gives you basic information for using a product and keeping it in good running order, a user's manual for people contains basic information about their character and the relevant behaviors they need to see from others in order to succeed in working with them.

This should make sense: people who are entering professional relationships with others often try to suss them out, discover what makes them tick, and shift their own behavior accordingly in order to obtain the best results. In some religions, pastors sit with romantic partners and help them to know one another as preparation for getting married. Most companies have processes for onboarding new CEOs, allowing these leaders and existing members of the executive team to get to know one another as well as their capabilities, priorities, and work styles.[2] What I'm suggesting is that we do this kind of due diligence much more thoughtfully and deliberately than is the norm, applying a core personality framework grounded in psychological science.

CRAFTING A USER'S MANUAL

ONCE YOU'VE PRACTICED USING the Personality Blueprint to understand others and their stable personality traits, creating a user's manual isn't difficult. Think about a relationship you've recently started building. Maybe it's with a new boss or team member. What kinds of specific behaviors should you embrace to best fulfill the other person's expectations and needs? How might you engage with the other person to communicate well, avoid conflict, manage it well when it does occur, and in general keep the relationship healthy, interesting, and on track? Your goal here is to create a list of key behaviors to adopt and avoid during your interactions, one that can guide you through the relationship's inevitable ups and downs.

To help you amass this list, I recommend building hypotheses around the following important areas. Ask yourself:

1. Which actions or behaviors will likely tick this person off, or alternately, please them?
2. How might I best motivate this person to do what I want? And how do I keep them motivated over time?

3. How might I best ingratiate myself with this person?

4. How can I best read this person's moods—the behaviors on their part that suggest that they are happy, sad, angry, and so on?

5. How can I best give this person constructive feedback so that they're likely to hear it?

6. In general, what does this person need out of our relationship by virtue of their personality?

7. What does it look like when this person is under stress? What are the visible signs of stress?

8. What kinds of challenges or circumstances will likely derail this person in the course of their work?

9. How much can I trust this person and how will I know when the person is betraying me?

10. Knowing myself, how much will this person's personality likely challenge me? What specific problem areas should I look out for and what steps might I take to mitigate them proactively?

Running through these questions will allow you to generate a list of basic ground rules that you can deploy to help navigate the relationship. This need not be a long list—even just three or four strong, insightful ground rules can make a big difference. Although these ground rules won't guarantee that you'll build trust and avoid conflict, they'll help you to please the other person, avoid or minimize conflict, and handle tensions productively when they do occur.

Years ago when I was working at a larger firm, I created a user's manual for a senior partner whom I'll call Bob. He was managing a client account I was on, and so for that client he was effectively my boss. We had been running into conflict in recent months, and the tension between us came to a head when he confronted me out of nowhere and aggressively demeaned my work. Despite this, I did want to preserve the relationship—I knew Bob was well respected, if not especially liked, by many in the firm and that it wouldn't be prudent to battle with him. As a senior partner, he wielded power over me and there could be some backlash. Beyond this, I had actually kind of gotten along with him previously and we had a few things in common. Nonetheless, he now was being a total jerk, and I needed a strategy.

Applying the Personality Blueprint to organize my thinking, I knew that Bob was extremely smart, a highly complex thinker who had the ability to quickly pick up even the most difficult concepts with ease (Box #1—Intellect). At the same time, he could be stubborn and even combative when it came to his opinions about everything from client service to politics and current events. He always looked like he was ready for a fight (Box #2—Emotionality).

Beyond being an effective organizational psychologist, Bob had distinguished himself as a leader and strong communicator—charismatic, engaging, articulate, and funny (Box #3—Sociability). More recently, his career success had gone to his head, and he seemed to fall for his own hype. The arrogance oozed out of him.

In terms of his drive and work style (Boxes #4 and #5), Bob was ambitious and cared deeply about his professional reputation. He sought financial success, not for its own sake but because he wanted to be known as a successful person in general. He also cared about family and community and wanted to be known as a good father and citizen. When it came to his work style, he was frustratingly perfectionistic about others' work but unstructured in delivering his own.

Considering my list of questions in light of these insights, I arrived at important ground rules that could guide my behavior going forward. Notably, recognizing that he could react aggressively if his key beliefs or opinions were challenged, I could try to avoid those and related topics if I could. It wasn't worth it to clash with him on these issues, and if I could avoid instigating an emotional flareup, our partnership would benefit.

Second, on occasions where a difference of opinion might emerge unexpectedly and I wanted to influence his thinking, I realized that I should continue to engage him rather than ignoring or repressing the conflict. As a highly sociable person, Bob values conversation and he likes to talk through areas of disagreement. He actually enjoys the verbal sparring. Shrinking back from potentially difficult conversations would only frustrate him.

That said, when engaging with Bob, I wouldn't try to convince him of the facts or the science, as that would be a dead end (third ground rule). Regardless of whether my logic was superior to his, he would automatically resist what I was saying because he was used to intellectual jousting, knew that he was good at it, and took pride in being the smartest person in the room. Given how stubborn and quick to argue he was, I also would avoid giving any impression that I was questioning his authority and instead convey points in ways that affirmed his competence and intelligence—fourth ground rule. Knowing how much he liked to win, I'd refrain from trying to win an argument with him and focus on achieving my desired results while making him *feel* like he'd won.

Finally, understanding that Bob was not an especially organized person and was unlikely to seek a regular cadence of update meetings with me, I wouldn't wait for him to reach out to me—my fifth ground rule. I would call him to get on his calendar, and I wouldn't read silence on his part as an intentional slight. Remaining mindful of Bob's personality would allow me to calibrate my own expectations, preventing me from becoming angry and initiating conflict.

LEADING TEAMS AND
ORGANIZATIONS BETTER

IN ADDITION TO DEVELOPING user's manuals for people you already know well, you can also use them as you're getting to know new people better. This is especially the case for people who are joining a new team. In 2022, a business executive whom I'll call Lauren was appointed chief marketing officer at a major retail chain. She replaced a longtime leader whom everyone knew but whom no one really thought was that good. It was clearly time for a change and people were excited to hear about Lauren's pending arrival.

As part of Lauren's onboarding, I conducted an executive assessment that outlined key aspects of personality and capability that would impact her ability to hit the ground running at the company. As discussed in Chapter 4, this included a series of scientifically valid and consistently reliable personality tests and a three-hour deep-dive interview during which I learned about her life story. As a result of the assessment, a few important points became clear. First, Lauren was exceptionally smart, creative, and strategic. She had all the right experience as well as the drive required to hit a home run in the role. She was well put together and carried herself well. Those traits, however, could sometimes be perceived as stoicism. She was almost too perfect: well prepared and saying all the right things, but somehow robotic. Everything was "just so" in what she said, how she dressed, how she comported herself. She never made a wrong move or got thrown off her game. It was all so . . . packaged, to the point that she came across as inauthentic.

Lauren's perceived inauthenticity would have enormous consequences for her ability to integrate into this company, which revered the kind of inspirational leaders often found in high-growth retail cultures. If people couldn't believe in her, how were they going to buy in to her leadership? The key was to lose the veneer and dial up authenticity. Lauren needed to let her hair down, drop an f-bomb here and there (my suggestion), and let people into her world. I advised her to create a user's manual for herself that others could use to understand who she *really* was, how they could succeed when reporting to her, how they could troubleshoot when things went wrong, what her hot buttons were, and so on.

As we created that user's manual, we realized it would be best conveyed by an accompanying story. To let her guard down and show authenticity, Lauren needed to reveal something about her life experience that demonstrated she was a real person. And so she did. About a month after joining the company, she held a town hall. With all of marketing and related functions assembled, she walked out onstage in jeans and a T-shirt (in contrast with her usual perfectly tailored pantsuits). She told the audience how she had grown up a tomboy and had struggled with mean girls throughout school. As she further related, her mother never really showed her how to put on makeup or dress in a feminine way. As a result, Lauren always thought she was ugly (it was so powerful to hear her say that). She recounted being bullied and made to feel less than her peers. Then, in an inspired way she described how she became determined to never let herself feel that way. She figured out how to dress well and present herself in a manner she thought would fit in. This growing attention to aesthetics and design was actually the genesis of her interest in marketing, and probably how she got to be the person she was today.

"I know," she said, "that sometimes I come across as overly polished or too rehearsed. I know it is my shield. What I want you to know is that there is a real person behind that, flaws and all, and I am grateful to be in the position to be leading you." Standing at the back of the auditorium, I could see people's jaws drop. The entire audience leaped to its feet in applause. What a moment. "So with that," she went on, "here is what you can expect from me. . . ." She described her leadership style, framed largely using the categories of the Personality Blueprint, and then discussed how she intended to approach her new role. In the days that followed, she told me how people approached her spontaneously and told their own stories. They spoke to her in a way that she had not seen before: personal, open, and very human.

I also often work with my clients to create user's manuals for entire *teams*, not just individuals on those teams. I do this in the context of team effectiveness engagements, whereby a senior team has asked me to help them raise their game and work better together. We hold a series of off-sites, and I'll also observe them as a team and conduct individual assessments to give team members feedback on their own contributions. As is fairly common in such engagements, one of the off-sites we do involves compiling individual personality assessment results and determining the collective impact of the team's personality constellation. When you look at personality test scores of individuals all layered on the same chart with their teammates, you get a collective team personality. One could argue that a team's collective personality is a reflection of its culture. If you describe a team, for instance, as composed of complex, analytical thinkers who are kind of shy and awkward with each other yet disciplined in tracking progress against objectives, you're in effect describing its culture. The same goes for a team of small-town, hardworking leaders who don't have much formal education but succeed because they work together well, tease each other in playful ways, and support each other through thick and thin. These are at once team-level personalities and culture.

The point of assessing a team's personality is to understand what it needs to do in order to raise its game. In the context of my work with teams, we take that team's personality and create a *charter* around it. This charter is a collection of team norms, dos and don'ts, and aspirational team behaviors. A team full of shy, analytic thinkers might have a charter that commits members to spend more social time together, talk about practical goals rather than theoretical ones, and make room for creative brainstorming at the end of all meetings. A team of small-town, hardworking leaders might have a charter that calls for adopting more sophisticated and structured management rhythms, holding each other accountable, not using humor as a way of deflecting difficult conversations, and committing to formal professional development. Putting up the mirror to a team, understanding its collective personality, and aligning around a team-level user's manual ultimately leads to high performance.

RESOLVING CONFLICTS WITH PARTNERSHIP ROAD MAPS

IN LATE 2020, I received a call from the chief human resources officer at a large health care company. Two senior executives at the firm—"Gerry," the general counsel, and "Charles," the CFO—were at war with one another. They tore into one another openly at meetings and griped about one another to others. Trust between them had broken down as each had learned from other senior leaders and board members that the other was bad-mouthing him. When I spoke with each of them, the core issue seemed to be a complaint on Charles's part that Gerry was bullying him. In particular, Gerry was aggressively claiming responsibility for issues that fell into Charles's domain and consulting with the board on them without his involvement.

Meeting with each of them and conducting informal assessments, I found that the two were quite different in character. Gerry
was a sharp, analytic thinker capable of understanding complex
issues, but he was also excessively logical, often arriving at conclusions that were technically correct but that failed to take human emotions into account. Having grown up in a tough Brooklyn
neighborhood, and having later worked in an investment bank with
a highly competitive culture, he had the personality of a bold and
brash courtroom lawyer. He was aggressive and blunt with people,
with no filter, telling them exactly what he thought without much
care for their feelings. If others didn't like him, he was fine with
that; he liked working independently and didn't rely on others in
his decision-making. As general counsel, Gerry harbored a strong
sense of duty to the organization, but in his zeal to do the right
thing he became arrogant and stubborn, failing to question his
own positions or consider others' points of view. He liked to be in
control, and as he had already risen to the top of his profession, he
seemed motivated to build an empire of influence for himself inside
the company. In terms of his work style, he was highly diligent and
detail-oriented, placing a high value on accuracy.

Charles was equally intelligent and diligent but in other respects quite different. Notably, he was much gentler in his demeanor. While he was hardly a pushover and no less confident in
his judgment, he tended to temper his messages to avoid offending
others. Charles could be combative, but he tended to adopt behavior that was more passive-aggressive. In line with his midwestern
roots, he often would hold back his real emotions in the moment,
cracking a sly, ironic smile when what he really wanted to do was
rant and rave. He was more collaborative than Gerry and in fact
struck me as a bit of a peacemaker. Although he was angry at Gerry,
Charles seemed more invested than Gerry was in finding a way to

move past their quarrels. He didn't seem as interested as Gerry in amassing power or authority. He didn't feel the need to mark his territory.

To help Gerry and Charles get along better, I facilitated a couple of sessions with them. Honestly, I don't love doing this kind of conflict management work because it is akin to couples therapy and often ends poorly. These sessions were important, though, given how critical Gerry and Charles were to the company. We had to give their relationship a shot.

After laying down basic ground rules for our conversation and establishing common goals, I had Gerry and Charles each convey his own narrative of the conflict between them, contemplate its causes, and expound on what each of them might do to move past it. Charles was visibly eager to set the relationship on the right track, while Gerry seemed to be reluctant but willing to accept a relationship reset. With my guidance, and bearing in mind what I had learned about each of their personalities, the two agreed on a set of ground rules they could use to guide their behavior going forward. I call such rules a "partnership road map"—essentially, a jointly created user's manual for the relationship.

Gerry and Charles both agreed to be honest with one another. The two would communicate directly rather than going behind one another's back and would take care to speak in ways that wouldn't diminish the other—a special challenge for Gerry, but one that he pledged to work on. The two would respect one another's expertise and authority, even when one of them was convinced that he was right on an issue and the other person wrong (again, particularly important for Gerry). Finally, the two would try to be more open-minded with one another, willing to entertain ideas that at first glance seemed misguided to them.

In addition to outlining these rules, the partnership road map

contained mechanisms for holding Gerry and Charles accountable. The two agreed to convey the key tenets of their agreement
to their respective teams as well as to several other top executives. These leaders would help to hold Gerry and Charles accountable, reporting to me whether they felt Gerry and Charles
were abiding by the agreement. These leaders would also refrain
from behaviors that ran counter to the road map, such as gossip-
ing with either Gerry or Charles behind the other's back. Gerry
and Charles agreed to check in with me about their performance
after three months and again after six months had passed. If you
create user's manuals for yourself and others around you, you can
inoculate yourself against harmful conflict. If you do find yourself
in conflict with someone in your orbit, mobilize the tools we've
discussed in this chapter. Of course, the creation of a partnership
road map is no guarantee that you'll be able to resolve issues you
have with others. Sometimes personalities clash too forcefully
to allow for a positive outcome. Likewise, all of us carry psychological baggage and fall into unproductive habits when stressed,
burned-out, or overwhelmed. The best way to deal with conflict
is to deal with it head-on. A shared partnership manual helps you
facilitate that.

While working with Gerry and Charles, I came to realize that
they probably wouldn't be able to salvage their relationship over
the long term. I suspected that Gerry's aggressive and at times
conniving behavior reflected some underlying personality traits
that would prevent him from getting along with anyone. Sadly, it
turned out I was right. Months later, he left the organization after
antagonizing others around him. A partnership road map can often
stabilize a conflicted relationship for a period of time, but in many
cases, the best solution might well be ending the relationship—for
everyone's sake.

HOW WELL DO YOU REALLY KNOW PEOPLE?

BUILDING AND SUSTAINING MEANINGFUL relationships requires a lot of work. It's about showing respect for others, communicating openly and honestly with them, respecting their boundaries, affirming their value in our eyes, and so on. But there's an even more basic strategy that we often overlook: taking time and effort to really try to know others and understand how they tick. In our fast-paced, digital society, we spend most of our time with our attention elsewhere, when in fact a great deal of what we need to know in order to live and work in harmony with others is right there in front of us. The tools I've presented—the user's manual and partnership road map—give us precisely that, allowing us to behave in ways that will support, affirm, and please not just people in general, but the specific people in our lives.

There's another reason to pay attention to personality in relationships. In Chapter 1, I told the story of Frank, the founder of a software company who wanted to step back from daily operations and hire a COO to run his business. Initially, Frank hired a candidate from outside the company whose personality made him a poor match for the job. When that leader didn't work out, Frank decided to replace him, this time with a leader who had grown up inside the company. He settled on Sonia, a strong leader who had helped to run one of the firm's portfolio of constituent businesses. Now Frank came to me with a new request. He was thrilled to have Sonia as his new COO and thought he would work well with her, but he wanted to make sure that their relationship started off in the best way possible. Would I coach them together during the first year to help them proactively address any potential issues that might arise?

After agreeing to help, I proceeded to conduct an assessment of Sonia. When I sat down for our three-hour interview, I wasn't expecting the assessment to be especially revealing. Sonia seemed very nice but not especially charismatic or colorful. She came across to me and others inside the firm as a no-nonsense kind of person—calm, levelheaded, smart, a solid manager. I began as I usually do, having Sonia talk about her present role and then delving into her past. When I asked her to name an early influencer of hers, she mentioned her grandmother. "What were your parents like?" I asked. Without warning, Sonia's demeanor changed. She grew silent, her body stiffening, her face becoming pale.

Sonia went on to tell me something that only a few other people in her life knew. When she was a little girl, her stepfather, a former drill sergeant in the military who had become a successful real estate developer, abused her and beat her to the point where she had to go to the hospital to receive medical treatment. Her mother, a drug addict, was out of the picture and unable to help. When Sonia was eight, other family members intervened, and Sonia's parents sent her away to boarding school. For the rest of her childhood, Sonia lived away from her family, seeing her parents only during the occasional holiday.

Despite the trauma of these experiences, Sonia managed to thrive in boarding school. She earned top grades and eventually gained admittance to a good college. She started working at a large tech firm right out of college and built a successful career for herself. For most of her adult life, Sonia blocked out what had happened to her, distancing herself from her family and focusing on living her own life. This strategy had worked until just a few years earlier, when the past finally caught up with her. While sailing in the Caribbean, Sonia suddenly and unexpectedly became flooded with emotions and broke down. She realized that she had to confront her stepfather about what had happened. She did so a few weeks later, hoping that he'd take responsibility for what he'd done. Sadly, he refused to do that. Sonia would have to process her emotions on her own and somehow find a way to forgive her stepfather so that she wouldn't feel tormented by her anger.

When I heard Sonia's story, I at first felt sick to my stomach at hearing about how cruel her adult family members had been to her. I felt so sad for Sonia that she had endured such trauma. Most of all, though, I was in awe of her resilience and felt inspired by her ability to survive her childhood and its horrors. Clearly, she was someone quite special. Reflecting on her personality, I felt certain that her early experiences had shaped it in some fundamental ways. Intellectually, she was not only decisive and firm when making decisions but placed a strong emphasis on fairness—understandable given how unfairly she had been treated as a child. She had a touch of ruthlessness about her, a determination to succeed at any cost that perhaps echoed the harsh, coldhearted way her father had treated her. Socially, Sonia took a calm, detached, unemotional stance that left people feeling they couldn't really get to know her well as a person. She had learned to compartmentalize her emotions early on and to keep people at a safe distance, and she was still doing it. She also was bold and willing to speak truth to power, which also made sense: after what she had been through, nothing in the workplace really scared her. She was highly ambitious and constantly eager to prove herself to others, perhaps because she had never felt a sense of validation from her parents growing up. In terms of her work style, she was highly tactical, responsible, structured, hardworking— habits she had likely learned in order to thrive in the demanding environment of a boarding school.

Hearing Sonia's shocking story affirmed for me the value of understanding what makes others tick. On the surface, Sonia came across as bland and unremarkable, even though she was undoubtedly a high performer. Her work colleagues had no idea about what had happened to her and the complex ways that it had shaped who she was, precisely because Sonia had taken such pains to repress her experience and prevent others from knowing about it. Now that I had unearthed this, I could help Frank and Sonia both adjust their behavior to improve their relationship. Since Frank, the prototypical entrepreneur, tended to be highly emotional and passionate and Sonia the very opposite, the two would have to work to create a common language that incorporated and respected both of their sensibilities. Sonia would have to learn to let her guard down a bit and express herself, articulating how she was feeling in the moment. Frank would have to respect Sonia's autonomy. He would also need to understand Sonia's underlying need for fairness and be almost overly even-handed and transparent with her. Further analysis of Frank's own personality would reveal still other ways that he could shape his behavior to avoid conflict and build trust with Sonia.

If Frank and Sonia had begun to work together the way most people do, they would have unwittingly headed for a collision of personalities. Each would have approached the relationship in ways that might have been ham-handed at best or destructive at worst—not because they intended to cause discomfort or harm, but because they didn't know better.

How well do *you* really know your boss, colleagues, spouse, and other important people in your life? How well do they really know you? Are people in your life hiding parts of themselves because it feels too scary or painful to bring them to the surface? Have you come to terms with your own past and how it continues to shape your personality? If you haven't delved into an analysis of personality and its implications, the people around you are likely mysteries to you, even if you think you know them well. You might even be a mystery to yourself. For the sake of your relationships, dedicate yourself to asking more questions. Lift your head up from your phone (or this book, just for a minute) and look at people. Really study them. You have so much to gain by cultivating perceptivity and allowing it to guide your actions, not just at the beginnings of relationships or at moments of conflict, but at any time.

KEY INSIGHTS

- We can use a knowledge of personality psychology not just to choose individuals as partners but also to manage work and personal relationships so that they start off well and stay on track.
- To manage relationships with people in your orbit, create a "user's manual" for each one, using the Personality Blueprint and the interviewing techniques described earlier in this book to systematically analyze who our relationship partners are and what makes them tick.
- Before attempting to create user's manuals for important people in your life, try creating one for yourself.
- In addition to deploying user's manuals to improve our relationships with others, we can also use them to improve our leadership of teams.
- When we clash with others, insight into personality coupled with a shared user's manual can provide us with powerful tools for helping us to resolve conflict and keep relationships on track.

Chapter 6

IMPROVING PERFORMANCE

IS YOUR PERSONALITY IMPEDING your own success? One executive I coached at a high-profile marketing agency whom I'll call Tanya found this to be the case. The company's CEO had tasked her and a colleague, "Samantha," to run a key business unit together as co-leaders. Although both women were smart and ambitious, Samantha was particularly exuberant, outgoing, and charismatic. She had received an MBA from Stanford and been a rising star at McKinsey before coming to the agency. Earlier in her life, she had been a competitive tennis player. Smart, engaging, and ambitious, Samantha occupied the limelight without even trying.

Tanya was eloquent and kind but quieter than Samantha and more passive. She had grown up in a nice part of London, England, as the daughter of caring Korean parents. She had one sibling, an older sister who was now a successful investment banker. In school, Tanya was bright but achieved only modest academic success. As Tanya told me during my formal assessment of her, she had been aware during her childhood of being "average" in many respects, never in trouble but never standing out academically or socially. She struggled as a result with a certain amount of anxiety. She had a few close friends growing up but was never invited to the cool-kid parties and typically stayed home on weekends. Her parents loved and nurtured her, perhaps even doing too much to shield her from the realities of the world.

When Tanya left home for university, she started to do better in school although she couldn't shake her underlying anxiety about being average. She had sought counseling for it years ago and had mostly prevented it from debilitating her, though it still seemed to linger beneath the surface.

Upon leaving university, Tanya got a job at the agency. Working hard, she found that she had a knack for marketing. She rose steadily through the ranks and had been appointed to her current executive role three years earlier. She was a lifer at the company, never having experienced working anywhere else. My assessment showed that she was, in fact, supersmart and loved complexity; she saw the world in a nuanced way that contrasted with Samantha's binary, black-or-white thinking. Tanya was also interpersonally sensitive, caring about others' welfare. She had a gentleness to her that people sometimes mistook for weakness. In fact, she was just as shrewd as anyone, driven by money and the satisfaction that came from landing lucrative deals. She simply maneuvered people and situations with more subtlety—a different personality. Despite her anxiety and a core need to be liked by others, she was outwardly calm and composed, nonconfrontational in an environment that fostered competitiveness. Along with that, Tanya could be fairly described as dispassionate. To her, succeeding at work was about drive, empathic leadership, and execution. She knew what she needed to do and did it.

Because of her reserved style, Tanya found that Samantha was most often the loudest voice in the room and got most of the attention and credit, including when it came to ideas that Tanya had generated. Tanya even felt that Samantha was playing bad politics and trying to box her out, hoping to outcompete her in their boss's eyes.

Over time, these feelings on her part tarnished the relationship between her and Samantha.

My job was to coach Tanya through this difficult terrain. Genuinely interested in raising her game, Tanya had to contend with a fierce competitor who was playing to win and backstabbing her in the process. To organize our work together, we identified two goals. First, we'd seek to elevate her as a leader by identifying gaps in her capability and shoring them up. Second, we'd navigate the tough terrain related to Samantha.

Our ability to achieve both of these goals hinged on a deep understanding of Tanya's personality. Although Tanya's understated temperament was endearing, she needed to work on generating more impact as a leader, especially at this agency. She could learn to speak more assertively, adopting a more strident, confident tone, interrupting others from time to time when the situation warranted it, sitting up straighter in her seat, challenging herself to set the agenda more intentionally in meetings rather than letting someone else do it, and so on. Tanya already had enviable skills as a leader, beginning with her sharp, strategic mind. The missing link for her was the ability to project executive authority.

Through extensive executive coaching over a two-year period, Tanya achieved more mastery over her interpersonal impact. She gained a sharper picture of the specific behaviors she naturally expressed, the subtle "tells" she gave that let others read her in certain ways. These included vocal tone and volume as well as her body posture, particularly when she was in the presence of strong personalities. When a powerful person or adversary leaned in, she tended to defer and physically recoil, becoming hunched over, quiet, slow, and flat in her tone.

We delved into the origins of these behaviors and what they meant psychologically, addressing the personality traits involved and discovering how Tanya might use them to have more of a positive impact. We had Tanya experiment with subtle and discreet changes in her behavior. In a meeting, she would talk louder and more quickly and then observe the reaction of those around her. Rather than offering a rambling answer, she would structure her comments more, using a strategy I call "speaking in threes." When she had a point of view, she would make statements like "I have three reactions to this. First . . ." or "The way I see it, we have three options. First . . ." This strategy allowed her to come across as sharper, more confident, and more authoritative.

All of this work eventually began to pay off. Over time, Tanya gained enough mastery over how she expressed her personality that she could dial her behaviors up or down depending on the requirements of the situation. She began to deal with Samantha more effectively and in general to express herself as a strong, high-performing leader. Samantha wound up leaving the organization, recognizing that she couldn't overshadow Tanya any longer. Meanwhile, Tanya's stock inside her organization soared. Her firm's CEO publicly acknowledged her great work on several occasions, including at board meetings during discussions about succession. She is now well positioned to become a high-profile executive in her field.

There are many self-help books on personal performance, some of them wildly successful, that focus on identifying specific behaviors we should adopt and helping us to make habits of them. As helpful as individual habits can be, they don't get to the underlying causes of leadership behavior, nor do they reveal levers to pull that might allow for real change. Each of us has important strengths and weaknesses on account of our personalities, qualities that influence how much success we can expect to achieve. Our biggest weaknesses might seem obvious enough to us, but aspects of our personalities that we regard as strengths can also, if taken to an extreme, hamstring our efforts. It's great to be agreeable around others, but if we're too agreeable, we become sycophants, saying or doing anything just to please others and make friends. It's nice to be passionate about what we do, but if we're too passionate, our unfettered enthusiasm can cause us to become easily frustrated, moody, irritable, and inclined to give up too soon on projects and people that disappoint us.

To really improve our behavior, it's important to understand what is truly behind it—the nuances of our personalities, how they were formed, and how we tend to express specific traits. We must dig deep and consider how our early life experiences influence who we are today. Otherwise, we'll adopt solutions that don't stick and work hard to change behavior over the short term only to find that in times of stress our unhelpful tendencies crop back up.

Mental health practitioners today are increasingly acknowledging the importance of going deep when treating mental health problems. Over the past two decades, practitioners adopted more superficial, HMO-driven treatments like short-term counseling and pharmaceutical treatments. When you go to your primary care physician and complain about having anxiety, your doctor immediately prescribes you Xanax or Celexa and hopefully refers you to a therapist. That therapist, who is slammed with a full client roster, suggests a six-session plan of cognitive behavioral therapy (CBT). In some cases, these treatments don't work (sorry, CBT friends!). Other experienced clinicians know that to treat a broad range of mental health conditions, you must explore the condition's genesis and underlying nature (hello, psychodynamic therapist friends!). Understanding the person and not just their symptoms leads to real treatment. In the same way, leadership coaching without an understanding of the whole person, their core personality traits, and how they came to be is just superficial advice-giving that won't lead to lasting performance change.

Even with a deeper understanding of our personalities, we can't hope to eradicate our worst impulses entirely—our characters are, after all, stable and mostly fixed. But we can take action to correct for our unhelpful tendencies or moderate their impact over time. The key is to become conscious of our traits and their impact, and then to work deliberately, as Tanya did, to tweak and refine them. We must develop a practical perceptivity about ourselves, one focused specifically around personal growth and performance improvement. As we understand more deeply how aspects of our personalities impede us, we can train ourselves not to devolve back to habitual patterns, even in times of stress. And by coaching others around us to do the same, we can help them to develop and grow as well.

DISCOVERING POTENTIAL GROWTH AREAS

HOW CAN WE IDENTIFY areas of our personality to work on with an eye toward enhancing our performance? It's a trickier task than it might seem. Leadership coaches and HR leaders sometimes employ personality tests to identify individual factors that impede our performance. One popular method, the Clifton-Strengths approach, created by the Gallup organization (formerly Strengthfinders), assesses how strongly people exhibit certain key talents or abilities. The methodology identifies thirty-four themes or types related to talents—"Activator," "Maximizer," "Includer," "Arranger," and so on—and helps people determine the precise combination of types that best describes them as individuals.

With this personalized analysis in hand, individuals can improve their performance by leaning in on their strong areas. "Most people are taught to work on their weaknesses—to fix them," Gallup asserts. "But instead, they should be learning how their strengths can overshadow their weaker areas.... You can achieve the highest levels of success only when you stop trying to be a *little bit good at everything* and instead hone what you are *naturally best at.*"[1]

CliftonStrengths holds obvious appeal. If we're trying to improve, it's more comforting to think about our strengths than to focus on our weaknesses. Unfortunately, CliftonStrengths doesn't stand up to rigorous scientific scrutiny as a valid measure of personality. The "themes" that CliftonStrengths purports to measure are essentially made up constructs with an unclear scientific basis and no publicized correlations to established measures of personality. I could find no peer-reviewed studies confirming the validity or predictive value of the CliftonStrengths assessment, nor does peer-reviewed evidence seem to exist linking scores on the CliftonStrengths assessment with work outcomes like being a more successful leader or achieving more financial success.

Perhaps the more glaring problem with CliftonStrengths is its underlying premise: that we can improve by focusing exclusively on strengths. This just isn't true. Imagine you're a competitive tennis player with a decent forehand and a weak backhand. Sure, you can improve your game by working on your forehand. But if you ignore your bad backhand, it will remain a glaring weakness. You'll never reach your highest potential. Ask any professional athlete, and they'll tell you that they're always working on improving their deficiencies in order to get better. To improve our performance at work and in life, we should consider the totality of who we are as people, leaning into our strengths but also identifying how and what parts of our character inhibit us and taking remedial action.

In addition to the general, qualitative assessment of character I perform using the Personality Blueprint, I help clients of mine grasp flaws or unhelpful parts of their personalities by using a quantitative tool that does have strong science behind it, an assessment called the Hogan Development Survey. Developed by the psychologist Robert Hogan and widely used across corporate America, this tool measures "the dark side of personality," broken down into "eleven patterns of interpersonal behavior" that we typically manifest when we're under strain. Left unaddressed, these "derailers," as Hogan calls them, "can disrupt relationships, damage reputations, and derail people's chances of success."[2]

Interestingly, Hogan took as his starting point personality disorders that clinically impair normal functioning. Someone with diagnosable narcissistic personality disorder has an inflated sense of themselves and an outsize desire to receive attention and recognition from others. Those with antisocial personality disorder behave callously, mistreating others, violating social norms, and even breaking the law. These and similar disorders, which reflect various combinations or bundles of traits in my Personality Blueprint, represent *extremes* in behavior. In everyday life, people can exhibit these same bundles of traits, albeit at a subclinical level, when they're under stress. For instance, we might call attention to ourselves in situations where that doesn't serve our purposes, or we might respond too harshly to our boss or colleagues when we're stressed. These personality-driven behaviors might not rise to the level of psychopathology, but they do affect our work performance. If you ignore them and just focus on your strengths, you'll continue to flounder or fail to progress as a leader. Understand and embrace your leadership weaknesses or derailers, and you'll accelerate your development without question.

None of us is perfect. We all have productive aspects of our personality and those that impede our success. Take me, for instance. Many years ago, I uncovered some of my own personality-drive derailers with the help of an extraordinary clinical psychologist named Esther Gelcer. I was in college at the time and struggling to motivate myself and stay organized. Dr. Gelcer delved into my early history and family dynamics, and we did some testing, including cognitive and personality assessments.

Over time, a clearer picture of my personality emerged. I scored high on the intelligence test (phew) and was a lateral, creative thinker by nature. I loved big ideas and had a natural ability to see things differently. I was also sociable but had interpersonal insecurities, so while I loved being around people and they saw me as outgoing, I sometimes felt awkward and not part of the group. I was kindhearted and empathic by nature. I was driven and ambitious to do big things and had a core desire for success. Importantly, I was low in diligence. I just did not like structure or process. I was late for things and couldn't stick to schedules. I had trouble managing money and paying basic bills. Basically, I was undisciplined (I hated that about myself, but it was true).

Looking back on my childhood, I could see that my lack of discipline had long encumbered me, preventing me from performing at my best. During middle school, I did unusually well in some subjects and bombed others. My math teacher told my parents that I would get the most difficult questions right and the easy ones wrong. I frustrated an English teacher by participating well in class but never doing my homework and always being late on assignments. I was also messy and never could keep an organized binder. I was extremely curious and loved to learn, but I was more interested in ideas, concepts, and puzzles than the details and organization of those ideas. In high school, I did well but mostly by relying on raw ability rather than effort. I won a scholarship and went to college brimming with confidence. What I hadn't anticipated was the impact that the relative lack of structure in a university setting would have on me. With so many distractions and nobody telling me what to do, my longtime difficulty with organization and discipline became a big problem.

Once I understood my default disposition, I could do something about it. I switched majors into one where I could do well by understanding concepts rather than memorizing details or adhering to a discipline that someone else defined. I found that I just naturally understood psychology and it came easy to me, and in turn I got great grades. I went on to earn my master's in psychology and then found a PhD supervisor who allowed me to pursue my own research interests in a new area that was different from his. Again, I was pursuing ideas and creating rather than trying to adhere to someone else's formula for success.

After finishing my PhD and publishing some innovative research, I found a job at a big-city firm with a traditional culture. It was not long before I found myself falling into old patterns. As an employee, I struggled to comply with administrative demands and to arrive at meetings on time. While clients really liked my work and wanted more, I hated filling out internal billing and expense forms and account managers found my lack of structure frustrating. While my disorganization wasn't as bad as it once had been, I just couldn't shake this aspect of my personality.

I realized that it was time to make some bigger changes. First, I decided to leave that firm and start my own. I knew in my heart that I would be a better boss than employee. If I could drive the agenda and create, I would be more successful. Second, I put systems in place to offset my lack of structure. My first hire was Dr. Katherine Alexander, who in addition to being an excellent consultant was much more structured and disciplined than me. Hiring her was one of the best business moves I have ever made. Ten years later, she became the SVP of operations for our leadership advisory firm, Kilberry, which was recently acquired by global firm Russell Reynolds Associates. In many ways, Katherine was the real reason that our firm had been so successful and able to expand the way it did.

At some point, I also realized that executive assistants were like gold for me. My assistant Kristen Scott helps structure my calendar and reviews my email inbox to ensure that nothing falls through the cracks. Although I continue today to push against the inherent aversion I have to structure and discipline, it doesn't affect my success. I've found myself relying heavily on schedules (yes, I am beholden to my Outlook calendar) and lead a much more disciplined life. With the help of people and systems, I have achieved a great deal in my business and personal life. I truly believe it is because I have come to know myself well, including the parts of my personality that would thwart me if left unchecked.

Not all of us have the time or money for formal testing, much less years of work with a therapist or coach. If that's the case, you can still begin to make progress by working with Hogan's model more informally. Below are my interpretations of his eleven derailers. By familiarizing yourself with them, or better yet evaluating for yourself through the Hogan Development Survey, you can identify those that seem most pertinent to you and take action to work on them.

HOGAN'S ELEVEN DERAILERS

1. **You're too excitable:** It's good to be passionate and enthusiastic about your pursuits, but take it too far and

you can become easily frustrated, moody, irritable, and inclined to give up too soon on projects and people that disappoint you. This derailer reflects traits captured in Dimension #2 of the Personality Blueprint, Emotionality. It's a nonclinical version of what psychologists call histrionic personality disorder and borderline personality disorder.

2. **You're too skeptical:** It's good to stay alert to signs of deceptive behavior in others and to take action when you detect it. Take that too far and you'll become cynical and mistrusting, with a tendency to hold grudges. In the workplace, people who are too skeptical also tend to be overly defensive and critical and preoccupied with organizational politics. This derailer reflects traits captured in Dimension #1 of the Personality Blueprint, Intellect, and is a nonclinical version of paranoid personality disorder.

3. **You're too cautious:** A little risk aversion helps us. Too much of it, though, and we become gripped by a fear of failure. Criticism from others will terrify us, and we'll react defensively when we receive it. We'll also behave in unassertive ways, leading others to overlook or ignore us and give others the credit. Given the links between risk and motivation, we can associate this derailer with Dimension #4 of the Personality Blueprint, Drive, but it also impacts elements of decision-making captured in Dimension #1, Intellect. We can think of this derailer as a nonclinical version of avoidant and dependent personality disorders.

4. **You're too reserved:** Excessively introverted people

often don't thrive in leadership roles or other social situations. Others might regard such people as aloof and removed, unconcerned with their feelings. Taken to the extreme, this behavior pattern would resemble avoidant personality disorder. The pattern corresponds to traits described in Dimension #3 of the Personality Blueprint, Sociability.

5. **You're too bold:** To thrive in your career, it helps if you can take bold action at the appropriate times. People who are too bold become overly confident and even arrogant. They become enamored with themselves, believing that they have unique gifts and are born for greatness. They have a hard time admitting their mistakes or learning from experience. If you've ever met someone with narcissistic personality disorder, you might recognize this behavior. It falls under Dimension #3 of the Personality Blueprint, Sociability.

6. **You're too willing to test limits:** Taking risks and breaking the rules allows us to make progress in our careers, but too much of this trait leads us to behave impulsively, erratically, and irresponsibly. Patients suffering from borderline personality disorder manifest these risk-taking tendencies, but taken to the extreme. Dimension #5 of the Personality Blueprint, Diligence, best captures the traits corresponding to this behavior (people taking such risks manifest a *lack* of diligence, organization, or rectitude).

7. **You're too engaging:** It's entertaining when we encounter fun, gregarious people in the workplace. Taken too far, these individuals can become distract-

ible, requiring constant novelty and stimulation. They also hog the limelight, preventing others around them from contributing. We can think of this behavior as bearing a resemblance to histrionic personality disorder, in which patients seek attention and express their personalities in excessive or flamboyant ways. It corresponds with Dimension #3 of the Personality Blueprint, Sociability.

8. **You're too diligent:** To get ahead, a capacity to work in a disciplined, focused way is vital—something we track in Dimension #5 of the Personality Blueprint, Diligence. Take such discipline and focus too far and you become perfectionistic, inflexible, overly concerned in the details, and too hard on people who in your estimation don't measure up. Nobody likes a boss or a partner who sets extreme standards and goals and who can't see the big picture. We can think of this behavioral pattern as related, at the extreme, to obsessive-compulsive personality disorder.

9. **You're too agreeable:** People who are loyal and dependable make for great teammates. Take it too far and you become a sycophant, saying or doing anything just to please others and make friends. Dimension #3 of the Personality Blueprint, Sociability, captures this sort of behavior. Clinically, extreme expressions of this pattern can show up as dependent personality disorder, in which patients experience a lack of self-confidence and feel excessively beholden to others.

10. **You're too much of an oddball:** The zany, creative, imaginative among us help us to innovate. Taken too far,

imaginativeness can lead people to become overly eccentric, self-absorbed, aloof, and lacking in social skills. They're able to see what others don't, but they don't take the time to edit their thinking so that others can understand and accept it. This behavioral pattern falls under Dimension #3 of the Personality Blueprint, Sociability. It relates to schizotypal personality disorder, in which patients typically think and behave eccentrically.

11. **You're too passive-aggressive:** It's great to think for yourself and not care too much about how others regard you. However, in some cases independent-minded people will perform tasks the way they want while giving others around them the impression that they are respecting their wishes. This behavior pattern, when taken to the extreme, might show up clinically as antisocial personality disorder. It encompasses a bundle of traits associated with Dimension #3 of the Personality Blueprint, Sociability.

Anyone who has ever worked in an organization will recognize one or more of these derailers. We've all come across sycophants, perfectionists, office clowns, thrill-seekers, oddballs, and others who behave in difficult ways. We know how annoying these people can be and how much they can disrupt our work. At the same time, we're likely much less attuned to how *we* might display some of these behavioral patterns. If we're struggling to perform better and don't know why, one of these derailers might be the culprit. And if we're already performing well but wish to achieve even greater success, thinking carefully about our behavior with Hogan's derailers in mind can help us to spot new opportunities for growth and development.

FROM SUCCESSFUL SALES LEADER
TO GLOBAL SPORTS EXECUTIVE

TO ILLUSTRATE HOW UNDERSTANDING our personalities can help us to improve our performance, I'd like to tell you about the greatest coaching success story I've ever had. Dave Hopkinson grew up in a middle-class family in Toronto. Although he was bright and got into a great college, like me he found himself somewhat unsure about what he wanted to do in life. Recognizing that he was good with people and enjoyed interacting with them, he decided to go into sales. His first job—selling tickets for the local Toronto Argonauts (known more affectionately as the "Argos") football team—was a brutal one. Although Canadian football had its fans elsewhere in the country, there weren't many of them in Toronto. To most Toronto-nians, the Argos were the equivalent to the local high school football team in most regions of the U.S.—that is to say, not such a big draw. I don't know how Dave did it, but somehow he managed to sell a lot of Argos tickets during his early days there.

Later, when the company that owned the Argos and the infinitely more popular Toronto Maple Leafs hockey team acquired Canada's expansion National Basketball Association franchise, the Toronto Raptors, Dave was assigned to sell their tickets. Again, he was ex-tremely successful. Over a twenty-year period, he rose up the ranks in the Raptors' parent company, Maple Leaf Sports & Entertain-ment, becoming widely known inside the organization by the en-dearing nickname "Hoppy." By 2012, when I first met Hoppy, he had established himself as a highly successful leader, overseeing all ticket sales and marketing partnerships—the moneymaking en-gines of any sports organization—for the company's growing port-folio of teams.

As I quickly realized, Hoppy was a master salesman—the best I'd ever seen. He not only had amazing street smarts but was highly sociable, passionate, energetic, and committed. He was also hugely ambitious, hardworking, and determined. He was incredibly curious and loved to learn. Everyone around him found him to be a strong, charismatic leader. He was a great guy, caring and compassionate, easy to befriend or follow. His ability to read others' personalities was off the charts. At the same time, like anyone, he still had room to grow in his career. He needed to cultivate more executive patience, CEO perspective, and strategic discipline to go with his unmatched sales, marketing, and people-related leadership skills. If he did, there was no limit to how high he might rise in the industry.

I was so taken with Hoppy's talents and growth potential that I did something I'd never done before or since: I invited him to go for lunch and asked if he'd be interested in having me coach him so that he could reach the next level of leadership success. Hoppy accepted my proposal, and we began to work together. I conducted a formal assessment, including both an extensive interview and a Hogan Development Survey. My assessment showed he had extraordinary strengths, in rare air on leadership capability. However, like all of us, he had room to grow. The survey confirmed my sense of Hoppy's key growth areas. He was *too excitable* as Hogan defined it—a bit too passionate in what he was doing, to the point that he could occasionally let emotions get the best of him. He could be *too engaging*, inadvertently directing too much attention to himself. In a similar way, his aggressive, high-energy charm made him a fantastic sales leader but prevented people from seeing him as a broader, strategic leader.

Hoppy needed to recognize that certain aspects of his personality that had once served him well would probably thwart him as he continued to advance. His spontaneous character worked well when he had to think on his feet as a sales and marketing leader, but now he needed to exercise new leadership muscles. Many organizations like a certain amount of steadiness and predictability, and as a senior leader he would need to provide that, including by making decisions more slowly and deliberately. To build followership as a CEO, Hoppy would need to communicate with more controlled gravitas. The point wasn't for him to tamp down his passion for the business at all, but rather to channel it to meet his objectives.

Over the next several years, Hoppy and I worked on these areas. We both knew, of course, that he would never change his personality in fundamental ways. Nor should he. To some extent, he would always be a strategic risk-taker, a charismatic leader who got results through sheer determination, passion, and extraordinary sports industry knowledge. By experimenting with specific behaviors, consciously observing others' reactions, and then developing new habits around the behaviors that had an impact, he could reach even greater leadership heights.

To come across well as a senior leader, Hoppy had to appear more measured—a leadership tweak that, in a subtle way, would also incline him over time to slow down his thinking and embrace a more disciplined decision-making process.

To round out his CEO perspective, he needed to gain more fluency in the operational side of the business and communicate in a way that a board of directors would want to hear. Finally, adding more predictable management systems would enable him to truly scale his leadership.

Hoppy's efforts to raise his game led to impressive growth on his part. Others around him began to notice him as a seasoned leader, someone who was not merely affable but operationally minded and also a strategic, thoughtful decision-maker. Before long, he catapulted to higher levels of success. In 2017, he engineered a deal whereby Maple Leaf Sports & Entertainment sold the naming rights to Canada's premier sports arena for $800 million, at the time the largest deal of its kind.[3] The following year, he left MLSE to become the global head of partnerships for the legendary soccer club Real Madrid, a position that would give him greater visibility in the industry and a global perspective. In 2020, he left to serve as president and then chief operating officer of Madison Square Garden Sports in New York City, parent company of the NBA's New York Knicks and the NHL's New York Rangers. It's one of the premier leadership roles in the sports business, and Hoppy deserves it. He is a truly extraordinary leader and person, beloved by many. If you ask me, his insatiable appetite for learning coupled with a deep understanding of himself and others is the real reason for his success. Yes, he is a brilliant dealmaker and an inspiring leader, but his perceptivity and ability to leverage insight about personality separate him from everyone else in his field.

DEFANGING YOUR DERAILERS

WITH HOPPY'S STORY AS inspiration, let's go back to Hogan's list of eleven derailers. Do any of them jump out at you as especially apt descriptions of you on your worst days? Look back on your childhood and your career, and think of your two or three greatest failures. How did these patterns contribute? If possible, show the list of Hogan's derailers to people close to you and ask for feedback about your behavior. What do they perceive are the biggest behavioral barriers to your success? Can they describe specific instances in which some of these behavioral patterns emerged most forcefully? How exactly are these patterns affecting your performance and inhibiting your success?

The goal here is to see beyond your habitual blind spots, improving your perceptivity as applied to *you*. As you start to think critically about your behavior and solicit feedback from others, spend time observing yourself as you go about your day. Notice behaviors large and small that seem to fall under one of the eleven behavioral patterns. Notice how others react when you exhibit these behaviors. Pay close attention to your behavior in situations when you're stressed, tired, hungry, or otherwise not feeling so great. What do you tend to do that alienates others and makes working with you more difficult? How does your own decision-making suffer in these situations?

As your derailers come into focus, link your analysis of them to a more general awareness of your personality and its origins as described earlier in this book. If you find that you're too excitable or skeptical, how did these patterns originate? What formative experiences or people in your life contributed to them? How did these patterns help forge your sense of identity and lead to the various choices you made along the way? How did they and other patterns intersect with one another to shape your experience and make you who you are? How did they manifest at earlier stages of your life? Did they always impede your progress, or were they relatively innocuous or even helpful during your childhood or early career? If the latter, what about your current context or your goals makes these patterns more damaging than they were before?

When you feel you've gained significant insight into your derailers, select two or three of them to work on. For each one, list the specific behaviors that you believe might be hurting you the most. Suppose you conclude that you're too diligent—your ingrained perfectionist tendencies are holding you back. After reflecting on your behavior and hearing what others think, you might include in your list behaviors like "I'm too demanding or judgmental when it comes to giving team members regular performance feedback"; "I'm too much of a micromanager"; "I stress out too much when it comes to giving presentations, endlessly revising my script because I want to get it just right"; and "I'm driving myself too hard, wasting too much time correcting even the slightest flaw." Or perhaps you decide that you're too reserved. In listing specific behaviors that trip you up, you might include the following: "I usually refrain from speaking in our weekly check-in meetings"; "I keep my camera off during Zoom calls"; "I start conversations without making small talk or asking how others are doing"; or "I don't say hi to others whom I pass in the hallway unless they say hi to me first."

Once you've listed these behaviors, consider which experiments you might try to help you soften or moderate problematic aspects of your personality. For example, if you're seeking to shift away from perfectionistic behavior, you might push against your tendency to micromanage by resolving not to offer teammates advice over a weeklong period but instead asking them how *they* think they might solve a problem. To prevent yourself from stressing too much about giving the perfect presentation, you might decide that for your next speech you won't write out the script for your remarks word for word but instead try merely sketching it out and improvising a bit.

Figure 5 below offers some sample behaviors you might try adopting to remedy each of the Hogan Development Survey's eleven derailers. I offer these primarily to spark your own creative thinking. You might well find it better to experiment with other behaviors, given the specifics of your personality, your unhelpful behavior, and the social context in which you operate. If you find yourself struggling to come up with promising behavioral experiments to try, think of people in your life who *don't* struggle with these particular derailers—who indeed are strong in these areas. What behaviors do they adopt that seem effective? Borrow some of these and try them out.

Tweaking our personality-driven behavior to improve perfor-mance is a gradual, iterative process. Don't hesitate to toss out be-haviors that don't feel right or that don't seem to have the desired impact. When behaviors do seem to work, keep doing them and also look for ways to refine those tendencies. If you're not working with a coach, see if you can at least involve colleagues, bosses, or others. When you experiment with new behaviors, debrief with others to see if they noticed a difference, and if they did, what impact it had. Use their feedback to tweak your behavioral experiments or jetti-son them if they're not working. If you can, see if you can check in with others around you monthly or quarterly to get their general impressions of your progress. Are you making meaningful strides? What advice do they have as to how you might continue to improve?

HOLDING UP THE MIRROR

WHEN I BEGIN COACHING clients, I often warn them to expect deep insights from me and a dose of tough love. Coaches often fail to help their clients because they lack enough context into their lives and don't push them hard enough. Seeking to be supportive advice-givers, they wind up functioning mainly as paid friends, providing comforting feedback and serving as a sympathetic ear but offering little else of value. Although having a paid friend can help clients handle crises and make short-term changes, achieving deeper, more enduring change requires that we cultivate an awareness of our per-sonalities with a specific eye to how they hinder us. As this chapter has argued, it's not enough to understand what we might do differ-ently in specific situations. We have to understand our habitual *pat-terns* of behavior, how they might have originated, how they connect

Derailer	Some Potential Behaviors to Try
"I'm too excitable . . ."	• Walk more slowly. • Deliberately insert pauses when you speak. • Speak more softly and try taking out some of the emotion in your speech. • Try to avoid gesticulating when you speak.
"I'm too skeptical . . ."	• Refrain from asking gotcha questions at meetings. Hold back even though you can probably poke holes in what others are saying. • When colleagues begin gossiping about others, walk away. • Focus on the positives. Not everyone is out to get you or lying to you because they want something. Embrace others' authenticity by believing their positive intent.
"I'm too cautious . . ."	• Challenge yourself to take one risk, large or small, every day, even if it's just trying a new dish, wearing a new look, or walking a new route to work. • When others propose ideas, don't dismiss them out of hand as too risky. Instead, ask for clarification on why the ideas might make sense.
"I'm too reserved . . ."	• Challenge yourself to start at least one conversation a day, asking questions and follow-up queries. • Each week, try to initiate a social engagement with at least one colleague or friend. • Challenge yourself to be the first person to speak in your upcoming team meetings.
"I'm too bold . . ."	• When you disagree or clash with others, set aside ten minutes to think about the situation from their point of view. • If you're leading a team, resist the urge to issue directives. Instead, make decision-making more collaborative by asking others for their thoughts. • Each week, set aside time to think about mistakes you made and how you might learn from them. Ask others for their input on how you might have handled certain situations better.

"I'm too willing to test limits . . ."	• The next time you break a workplace rule, openly acknowledge your transgression and take responsibility. • If you're tempted to react quickly to something disturbing that has happened, wait an hour before taking action (for example, sending an email or making a phone call). • Before making important decisions, challenge yourself to identify and analyze the pros and cons.
"I'm too engaging . . ."	• In team meetings, make a practice of staying silent until others have had a chance to speak. • When partnering with others on assignments, ask them to take the lead. • Look for opportunities each day to sing someone else's praises or give them credit.
"I'm too diligent . . ."	• Experiment with standards of "good." Nothing is perfect; the key is to recognize when something is good enough and then move on. • Identify your top five work priorities for the next six months. Avoid spending time on tasks that don't advance these priorities. • Delegate. Consider five tasks right now that you could delegate to someone else.
"I'm too agreeable . . ."	• Raise your hand and speak up at least once each day when you disagree with something. • Challenge yourself to ask more critical questions in meetings. • Make some small moves to "be yourself" more at work—for instance, by wearing a less muted outfit or by referencing parts of your life you've refrained from discussing.

"I'm too much of an oddball . . ."	• Slow down your speech, paying closer attention to others' reactions. • When offering your thoughts, pause and ask others if they're still with you or if they have any questions. • Before sending important texts or emails, hold off for an hour. Reread your message, thinking of ways to make it more appealing to your audience given their needs.
"I'm too passive-aggressive . . ."	• Avoid grudges or hidden rivalries. If you have a beef with someone, tell them so directly. • When you've agreed on a plan of action with your boss, check with them directly before deviating significantly from the plan. • When you offer feedback, avoid the "sandwich" approach in which you offer praise before and after making a critical observation. Just tell the person what you've observed and the impact it had. Be direct and objective about it.

Figure 5: Derailer Behavior

with other themes in our lives, how they impede our efforts. My job as a coach is thus to hold a mirror up to my clients, showing them the unvarnished and sometimes unpleasant truth about their patterns so that they might accept and work with them. You can hold such a mirror up to yourself. It's not always easy, but remember, we all have dark sides to our personalities. If you can bring yourself to acknowledge your less flattering behavior patterns and ponder how they came to define you, you can defang them, preventing them from determining your destiny.

Uncovering root-cause rather than surface-level insights about our derailers enables us to truly grow. Uncovering difficult aspects of our personal history and how they affect our personalities can sometimes feel scary or overwhelming. Inevitably, though, it can allow us to become more mature, integrated, and authentic human beings.

Chandra, a senior vice president at a large media company, was on the fast track to success. Having impressed her bosses with her commitment, hard work, managerial skills, and ability to execute, she seemed poised to rise one day into a senior leadership role. There was just one problem: she lacked a strong executive presence. As senior leaders at her firm told me, she seemed far more comfortable collaborating with junior members of her team rather than with her bosses. In important meetings with senior leaders, she could become emotionally reactive and easily frazzled. She often had trouble expressing herself, seeming wordy and unfocused. She didn't seem all that comfortable building relationships with senior leaders, often missing out on opportunities to socialize with them and get to know them better.

For years, Chandra tried to address this feedback by focusing on empowering herself as a woman leader. Someone had recommended Sheryl Sandberg's book *Lean In*, and Chandra did her best to internalize its lessons by projecting more confidence and authority at work. All she had to do, she thought, was somehow be more assertive and take charge. And yet, something still wasn't clicking. Others around her continued to take credit for her work and to overpower her in management team meetings. The problem was that Chandra hadn't developed enough self-understanding. It was one thing to understand intellectually the importance of leaning in and projecting confidence, but Chandra hadn't yet probed the specific psychological barriers that she faced when attempting to do so. She couldn't understand *experientially* what leaning in would mean to her and her life.

As I worked with Chandra and helped her to uncover aspects of her personality that were derailing her, important insights soon emerged. Chandra wasn't behaving like a senior leader not because she lacked the skills or temperament, but because she didn't *see* herself as one. And the reason she didn't had to do not merely with her experiences as a woman in the workplace, but with her own, unique upbringing. Chandra had grown up in a modest household. People in her family weren't successful leaders; they tended to be average in terms of their skills and educational performance. That was the message Chandra received at home: it's okay to be average, someone who doesn't stick out in a crowd.

When Chandra had gone to school, she didn't try to rise to the top. Although she was bright, she was content to get decent grades and not draw attention to herself on account of her excellence as a student. She didn't feel comfortable being "different," even if the basis for this difference was positive. It didn't help that she was tall in stature, towering over her peers. She learned to shrink down her body posture in an attempt to blend in with the crowd. As time passed, Chandra internalized the messages from her family, believing that she really was unremarkable as a person and incapable of ever achieving excellence.

Chandra's self-concept persisted through adulthood, and it continued to color how she behaved on the job. During one of our conversations, she remarked that many leaders at her company had expensive luxury cars parked in the company lot. But she didn't see herself as a "fancy-car kind of person." Although she might have enjoyed the comfort of a luxury vehicle, she was content to drive something far more ordinary. In truth, she didn't feel that she *deserved* to drive a luxury car. She wasn't all that special, she thought, and she shouldn't allow herself to project an elite image. No surprise that she became frazzled when interacting with senior leaders and had trouble being herself.

Chandra embarked on a number of behavioral experiments, the most notable of which was to actually purchase a luxury car (she could easily afford it, so this wasn't a stretch). The experience of sitting in that car and driving it proved pivotal, helping her to shift her image of herself. For the first time in her life, she began to think of herself as a real executive—someone who deserved to be in the C-suite.

Not long afterward, Chandra's behavior at work began to change. She became less tentative and more assertive. She felt more self-assured dealing with senior leaders and was able to express herself more clearly around them. It wasn't owning a nice car per se that made the difference. It was owning her position as an authority figure. Chandra already wielded power inside her organization. She just didn't feel comfortable doing so because of what she had heard in her youth. The car served as a metaphor for her accomplishments and position of authority, and she needed to own both in order to really elevate herself. Over time, she got used to the idea of having a nice car (a gorgeous Mercedes that she keeps immaculate). More meaningfully, she came to feel just as important as her colleagues around the executive table.

The notion that Chandra's own enduring self-concept was serving to entrench her unhelpful patterns struck her as a real epiphany. She had never connected these dots in her life before. Without realizing it, she was still operating under assumptions about herself and the world that she had lived with since childhood. Now that she was an adult, she could choose to challenge these assumptions and modify the behavioral patterns that they supported. This is how true development happens.

We might not be able to change our personalities, but we can certainly learn to understand them better. And that heightened awareness—that perceptivity—is everything. If you look hard at the behavior patterns that derail you and analyze where they come from, you can learn strategies for controlling and transcending those patterns, including when you're under stress.

More fundamentally, you can learn to feel more comfortable and genuine in your own skin. You can own your limitations just as you do your strengths. You can confidently change—while connecting even more deeply with the person you've always been.

KEY INSIGHTS

- To improve performance, it's not enough to identify specific behaviors to adopt. We must also understand how parts of our personality are hampering our success.
- Although we can't fundamentally change our personalities, we can adopt strategies to moderate or compensate for unhelpful parts of our character.
- To discover potential growth areas, we can't just look for our strengths. We must also identify the weaker sides of our character.
- Working with Hogan's eleven derailers, we can cue into behavioral patterns that might be holding us back.
- Enhanced self-awareness can help our performance—and enrich our lives.

Chapter 7

INFLUENCING OTHERS

YOU'RE DRIVING TO THE grocery store, stopped at a stop sign and about to make a right-hand turn. Looking to make sure nobody is coming from your left, you make the turn. You hear tires skidding, see a blob in your peripheral vision, and just as you're hitting the brakes you feel a car crashing into your left front headlight. The impact, which pushes your car a few feet to the right, leaves you shaken but unhurt. After taking a few deep breaths, you edge over to the side of the road and get out of your car to inspect the damage. The driver in the other car, a man in his midthirties, pulls his car off in front of yours and gets out, too. He appears unhurt, but his car is pretty banged up. You find that there is some significant damage to your car, too.

As the shock wears off, you feel pretty certain that the other driver went through a stop sign and was at fault. Glancing at the other driver, you wonder how you should engage with him. Should you stay quiet, asking him for his contact information but otherwise remaining aloof? Should you take an aggressive posture, letting him know in no uncertain terms that you think he was at fault and demanding his contact information? Should you try to work through the problem with him in a matter-of-fact way, coming to a consensus about what happened and how to proceed? Should you come across as friendly and make jokes about the situation? You want to make sure the other driver isn't hurt and call for help if he is. You also want to make sure that you have the proper documentation if he was at fault. And you're on guard, as you don't know anything about this stranger's mental state and whether the accident will trigger road rage.

Previous chapters have applied perceptivity to the tasks of selecting people, managing relationships, and improving performance, but you can also use insights about character in the moment to favorably influence others so that they behave as you wish. In high-pressure situations, even limited data about others and their personalities can give you a marked advantage.

Consider how hostage negotiators approach their work. Decades of research in forensic psychology have taught us that criminals disproportionately have antisocial personality disorder—they are, by definition, "grossly selfish, callous, irresponsible, impulsive, and unable to feel guilt or learn from experience and punishment."[1] Armed with this knowledge, negotiators can refrain from doing anything that challenges the hostage-taker's ego, as that will likely escalate the situation. They can refrain from appearing uncertain, since people with antisocial personalities will spot where they have wiggle room and try to manipulate it to their advantage.

Experienced negotiators likewise know not to expect antisocial hostage-takers to develop empathy or emotional attachment with their hostages, so delaying or otherwise passing time just doesn't help. Moreover, antisocial personalities have little underlying anxiety and are usually quite calculated in their thinking; they tend not to behave impulsively or out of panic. As a working assumption, negotiators can feel free to take unwavering stands and build ego-driven rapport with hostage-takers.[2] In all of these ways, an approximate profile of the offender serves police as a useful starting point. As negotiations proceed, they can fine-tune their knowledge of the offender and make adjustments, leading, hopefully, to a peaceful resolution.

Similarly, government leaders often benefit from understanding the personalities of their foreign counterparts. For decades, a group within the Central Intelligence Agency called the Center for the Analysis of Personality and Political Behavior has profiled the personalities of world leaders, including dictators like Saddam Hussein and Kim Jong-il, giving U.S. government officials actionable insights they could use when conducting diplomacy.[3] One of the most consequential uses of personality insight in international affairs took place during the 1978 Camp David negotiations between Israel and Egypt hosted by U.S. president Jimmy Carter. In advance of the summit, Carter tasked the CIA with helping him understand the personalities of the two primary parties to the negotiation, Israel's Menachem Begin and Egypt's Anwar al-Sadat.

According to CIA analysts, Sadat was a narcissist invested in establishing a legacy for himself. He was relatively uninterested in the details of the negotiation and wanted most of all to make a splash on the world stage by coming to a deal. Begin, by comparison, was obsessed with the details, suspicious as he was of the other side's motives.

Based on this insight, the CIA developed a strategy and tactics that Carter could deploy to steer the talks in a constructive direction. He wound up convincing Begin to leave the details to subordinates and join Sadat in focusing on larger issues. The resulting discussions led to a breakthrough and an enduring peace between Israel and Egypt.[4] Afterward, it became routine for the CIA to prepare such profiles for U.S. leaders before major summits.[5] Other governments likewise perform analyses of our political leaders. During the administration of Donald Trump, for instance, governments capitalized on his widely known ego and self-interested personality, adopting tactics like writing him "love letters," publicly praising him, and staying at his hotels.

In assessing foreign leaders, the CIA has a difficult job—they're seeking insight into people who might possess a wide range of relevant traits and who also might be practiced in revealing their character selectively or putting up a false front altogether. Fortunately, the CIA has the time and resources to undertake an exhaustive analysis, drawing from a wealth of publicly available material and consulting with people who have dealt with these leaders. When we're dealing with people in our everyday lives, including strangers we've just met, we might have little inkling at first into who they are. Most of the time we won't have an hour or even fifteen minutes to gather data and come to a reasonably detailed and accurate assessment of their personality, as described in previous chapters. We might have only a few minutes or even seconds. Is the science of personality helpful here? Is there some way to quickly size up people, arrive at working hypotheses of their personalities, and frame our reactions accordingly?

Indeed there is. Rather than attempting a rigorous personality assessment of the person before us, we can perform what I call a **Character Quick Take**, looking over the course of a few seconds or minutes to ascertain which bundle of personality traits is *most dominant*. Calling to mind the Personality Blueprint, we can stay alert for subtle clues in behavior or speech that indicate which specific traits other people lead with. Once we identify a leading trait, we can then adjust what we say or do in ways that might favorably nudge the other person to think or do as we wish. And as the moments pass and we gain new information, we can then confirm our initial impressions or refine them, changing in turn how we behave.

THE CHARACTER QUICK TAKE

- Stay alert for initial personality cues, calibrating for context
- Review your options
- Confirm, revise, or deepen your hypothesis
- Take action

Consider the fender-bender scenario. As you begin to interact with the other driver, you might spend just a few seconds or more chatting them up with an eye toward learning any revealing details about them from what they say or how they say it (tone of voice, accent, speed at which they talk, and so on). You might quickly determine that the driver's name is John and that he is extremely articulate and bright (he's speaking quickly and using a large vocabulary, for instance). Hypothesizing that he leads with the first category of the Personality Blueprint, Intellect, you might try to engage him by inviting him to problem-solve with you and focus on immediate, practical steps you can both take.

Or let's say John seems friendly and approachable, even in this unusual situation. Hypothesizing that he leads with Sociability, you might try to make a friendly connection with him, making small talk about your own life, before moving on to address the circumstances at hand.

Or let's say that John's tone of voice or reaction suggests that he is a sensitive person and genuinely worried about your welfare. Hypothesizing that he leads with Emotionality, you might try to make your own emotions more visible, expressing your shock or anxiety at what happened or your relief that nobody was hurt.

Character Quick Takes are no substitute for the deeper analysis of personality. They are prone to error, so if the situation permits, we should always take the opportunity to gather data and probe personality in a more comprehensive way. Still, relying on Character Quick Takes in spontaneous, potentially charged situations dramatically increases the likelihood that we'll handle the situation more productively. By applying the lens of perceptivity and orienting ourselves toward trying to understand others, we can behave in ways that might resonate better and allow us to get more of what we want—not every time, but fairly often. As we become more practiced at performing Character Quick Takes, our accuracy will likely improve, and with it, our ability to wield influence. At the very least, getting in the habit of quickly apprising character keeps us hyperattentive to perceptivity, enhancing our ability to practice good judgment in the bigger, more considered decisions we might make.

STAYING ALERT TO THE CUES

IN THE MOVIE *THE Bourne Identity*, Jason Bourne, the unwitting CIA agent whose amnesia has blocked out his identity, sits down in a restaurant with a new acquaintance. In explaining his bewildering sense that he is someone else, he wonders out loud why he is so alert to his surroundings. "I come in here," he says, "and the first thing I'm doing is I'm catching the sight lines and looking for an exit. . . . I can tell you the license plate numbers of all six cars outside. I can tell you our waitress is left-handed and the guy sitting at the counter is two hundred and fifteen pounds and can handle himself. . . . Now why would I know that?"[6]

We've discussed in this book how to elicit data in social situations and glean insights about character. When it comes to influencing others (usually strangers) during relatively brief, spontaneous encounters, I'd like to emphasize the importance of cuing in to even the smallest details of how people speak, act, and present themselves. We aren't all trained CIA agents who forget our true identities, but we still can maintain what cognitive scientists call "situation awareness," staying alert to the data about people that in fact is all around us. Professional poker players do this all the time. Sitting around the table, they look for the tiniest gestures—whether other players make eye contact, whether they respond quickly or slowly to gameplay, whether their hands shake, how chatty they are, what they're saying—to glean other players' emotional states and the kind of hand they're likely to be holding.[7] With that information, they can make more informed and hopefully successful decisions about whether and how much to bet.

Expert negotiators also know to read verbal and nonverbal cues to stay in touch with emotions. In recent years, academic experts and practitioners alike have recognized how important it is to be attuned to the emotional states of your negotiating partners.[8] Alison Wood Brooks, a professor at Harvard Business School, acknowledges how valuable it is to track others' emotions in negotiations, advising not only that negotiators "tune in to [their] counterpart's body language, tone of voice, and choice of words," but clarify emotions with others when their body language doesn't appear aligned with what they're saying.[9] People who are more adept at recognizing emotions accurately achieve better results in negotiation situations than those who don't.[10]

It's important that we pay extremely close attention, for emotional cues sometimes last only a fraction of a second. When people are speaking plainly with nothing to hide, they typically express individual emotions for up to four seconds—what pioneering psychologist Paul Ekman called macro-expressions. But sometimes people aren't being entirely straight with us. In these situations, they might still betray how they really feel via slight, almost imperceptible facial expressions that last as little as a thirtieth of a second. These "micro-expressions," as Ekman calls them, convey basic emotions, such as fear, disgust, or happiness. Pay close attention to micro-expressions and you can get a window into true emotions, beliefs, and character, helping you exercise good judgment and deal with others in more informed ways.[11]

And yet, as useful as recognizing emotions might be in negotiations and other spontaneous situations, I'm suggesting here that we scrutinize verbal and nonverbal cues in a different way—as a means of gleaning core personality traits (perceptivity), not superficial and fleeting emotional states (emotional intelligence). If someone is resisting a nuanced point we're making, is it because they're frustrated in the moment or because they're temperamentally given to narrow, black-and-white thinking? If we're in a sales situation and a customer is chatty, happy, and positive with us, is this because they like what we're selling or is that just their habitual style, the way they interact with most people? These are just a few of the many questions we might ask when seeking to probe beyond superficial emotions to understand core personality.

Such questions are critically important to pose, since knowledge about personality can often help us respond better than the mere awareness of an emotion can. If we think someone is feeling angry, stressed, or distracted, we might try to soothe them in the course of trying to convince them to believe or act as you wish. We might adopt a calm tone with them or empathize with what they're feeling and then express our point of view or make a request of them. But if we know someone is an angry *person* or that they gravitate toward black-and-white thinking, we might not even try to convince them of our point of view—that effort simply will not work. Similarly, if in a sales situation we think someone genuinely likes what we're offering, we might try to push the sale even harder or try to interest them in products or services. If we know that they tend to be chatty, happy, and positive by nature, we might take a more measured approach so as not to come across as too pushy or aggressive.

Wharton organizational psychologist and author Adam Grant has discussed the importance of understanding others' personality when attempting to persuade them. In his book *Think Again*, Grant conveys how hard it is to influence others to think differently, often because of their hardwired personalities.[12] Arrogance, stubbornness, and narcissism all make it more difficult to change people's minds. Ignore these personality traits and you'll feel endlessly frustrated as you encounter seemingly immovable opinions in others. Conversely, if you fail to pick up that a person is open-minded, even-tempered, and eager to question their own beliefs, you might find that arguing too forcefully for your position backfires—you come across as too arrogant, stubborn, or narrow-minded yourself.

At a recent dinner I attended, a physician friend of mine started to rant about "woke" culture, speaking with an intensity that I have rarely seen in him. To an eavesdropping diner beside us, he might have appeared to be an angry, emotionally charged person with whom rational debate was impossible. I could imagine such a diner either writing off my friend with a disgusted wave of the hand, or on the flip side, shouting his disgust at him and trying to overpower him with opposing rants.

I knew that my friend was a measured person, intelligent and oriented toward rationality. Based on that judgment, I chose to engage him substantively on the issue at hand. I dissected his arguments in a serious, evenhanded way, making arguments that were objective, reasonable, informed, and difficult to refute. I'm not sure if I won him over, but I do know that he listened and at least tested some of his own assumptions. The spirited conversation between us strengthened our relationship rather than eroding it as political debates often do.

Proceeding in this way won't work with everyone, but knowing my friend's personality was critical to my strategy. The next time you find yourself in a political conversation with someone you don't know well, look for behavioral cues related to personality. If they tell you that this person might be open-minded and susceptible to persuasion, go for it. Otherwise, you might think twice about whether to engage them.

A PERSONALITY CHEAT SHEET

IT CAN BE DIFFICULT or even impossible to separate emotional traits from core personality traits, but it behooves us to try as best as we can. When we first encounter others, we can observe their behavior and come to quick, initial impressions of their personalities. Although these impressions are susceptible to cognitive bias, research suggests that they are in fact often *right*.[13] One study asked participants to look for a split second at images of candidates for governor and Senate, including both the politician who had won a given race and the one who had come in second. On this basis, respondents were to choose the better, more competent politician. The majority of the time, these judgments about competence predicted the actual outcome of gubernatorial and Senate contests.[14]

To come to quick, initial judgments about personality and the parts of it that are most pronounced or that people lead with, it can help to look for a few of the most common cues for each dimension of the Personality Blueprint—what I call my "personality cheat sheet." When it comes to Box #1, Intelligence, I look first to language. What kind of vocabulary is the other person using? Are they uttering sophisticated words and using correct grammar? What hints do they offer about their job or career? If you discern that someone is a doctor or professor, for instance, you can infer as a working hypothesis that they possess above-average intelligence. Language might also shed light on other aspects of intelligence, such as how worldly a person is (are they talking about varying cultures or areas of inquiry?), whether they think in black or white terms (are they making categorical statements?), whether their thinking is logical and linear (are they veering all over the place in what they're saying?), and how curious they are (do they ask lots of questions?).

When it comes to Box #2, Emotionality, tone of voice matters. Is the other person speaking calmly, with a notable lack of emotion, or is their voice, on the contrary, wild and expressive (for instance, is their tone variable, with lots of shifts in volume and emotional tenor)? Are they focused on people in their speech, using *I*, *you*, and other pronouns, or do they focus on ideas or issues? People who lead in emotionality tend to focus on people and their subjective experience. Nonverbals also help here. Are their facial expressions exaggerated? Do they emit high-pitched laughs or other sounds? Is the person sweating profusely in a setting where temperature isn't a factor and the average person wouldn't be especially anxious? If so, or if they're fidgeting a lot, or if they're shrinking back in their seats and speaking softly, it may be that they are unusually anxious by temperament—a dimension of emotionality.

To tap into Box #3, Sociability, I pay attention to a person's interpersonal impact. Does an individual make eye contact often and easily? How loudly do they speak? Do they smile and laugh a lot or are their facial expressions more subdued? Do they appear comfortable meeting me or are they cautious and contained? Do they answer my questions substantively or just offer simple, one-word responses? Do they keep their distance from me, standing far away and positioning themselves away from me, or do they seem more comfortable? Do they make physical contact—say by reaching out to shake my hand or touch my arm—or are they standoffish?

To spot attributes related to Box #4, Drive, pay attention to how eager or aggressive people seem to be. If they're taking risks in conversation and trying to one-up you, it may be that they're competitive by nature and motivated by winning. On the other hand, if they're wearing flashy clothes or are loud and boisterous, they might be motivated by receiving recognition from others. If they're driving a flashy car, perhaps they're motivated by the prospect of amassing wealth. If they're dressed conservatively or are wearing jewelry with religious themes, religious values might matter to them and motivate their actions.

As regards Box #5, Diligence, other aspects of a person's attire can serve as a useful cue. Are they dressed neatly, with every last hair in place? For that matter, how about their office or personal space? Is that highly organized? Are they on time or do they rush in fifteen minutes late to your meeting? Do they seem to have a keen memory for specific details? That might say something about their intellectual capacity, but it might also suggest an attentiveness to detail that contributes to diligence. If they carry a purse, is it highly organized? Have they come prepared for every possibility (tissues in case they need to sneeze, snacks in case they're hungry, and so on)?

As you attend to these cues during the initial seconds of encountering someone, remember: you're not trying to immediately discern everything about them. These are undoubtedly—and intentionally—superficial observations that do not capture a person's real essence. For example, you might find that a person you meet arrives late or appears shy. If you got to know that person over time, you might find that these behaviors arise only in certain situations and that other, seemingly conflicting behaviors overshadow them. Taking your initial impression as your final, comprehensive judgment would be an obvious mistake. Likewise, these initial observations are prone to overgeneralization and can even lead to discrimination. You can't infer the essence of a person's character just because they dress a certain way or use a certain vocabulary. Again, the point here isn't to distill a person's full essence. You're just looking to achieve an advantage by identifying the most *prominent* trait or bundle of traits, the ones that the person leads with.

Make sure to calibrate your impressions to account for the social or cultural context. Our notions of context can cue us to expect certain traits before we even engage, allowing us to quickly test and refine our impressions. What begins as a mere stereotype on our part can in short order become a more substantive and reliable judgment. If we're interviewing at a technology company, we might presume that most people we meet lead with Dimension #1—Intellect, in that they're analytical and even a bit nerdy. When we encounter specific individuals, we can confirm that this is true or note when it *doesn't* seem to be true. Either way, our awareness of our own expectations leads us to better insight about character as our preconceived notions come up against the people standing before us.

A good deal of the time, attention to context can also allow us to avoid making interpretive errors. If we're visiting a corporate office and everyone is dressed formally, we probably wouldn't want to interpret the suit and tie worn by the person we encounter as evidence of an especially diligent, buttoned-up demeanor (Box #5). If we're at a funeral and everyone is sad and grieving, the person we interact with might not be introverted or shy simply because they're speaking softly and not making much eye contact with us (Box #3, Sociability). If we're on a late-afternoon sales call and the person sitting across from us seems distracted and harried, it may not be that they're a disorganized person (Box #5) but rather that we caught them at a bad time—they're getting ready to leave work for the day and are trying to wrap up a bunch of loose ends.

More generally, remember that any cue we seek to read might be susceptible to multiple interpretations. If we're at a rock concert and everyone else is wearing T-shirts and jeans but the person we encounter is sweating it out in a suit and tie or formal dress (I have seen this, and it is hilarious), that might suggest either a conversative bent (Box #4) or perhaps a social awkwardness or discomfort (Box #3). On the other hand, maybe we're on a group trip and they didn't know what was planned, even though three emails had been sent about it. In that case, their dress might suggest disorganization (Box #5). When thinking about context, consider its nuances and implications as fully as possible in the short time available to you.

Likewise, the fact that someone offers us a firm hand to shake might suggest that they are extraverted or collaborative and that they lead with sociability (Box #3).[15] But if that hand is unusually sweaty, we might think that they're anxious or lacking in self-confidence by temperament (Box #2). If that handshake is excessively firm, we might think they're trying to establish dominance, perhaps suggesting competitiveness on their part or a tendency to value physical strength and traditional notions of masculinity (Box #4). We should trust our initial impressions of a given cue, looking for additional signs that would suggest one interpretation over others. Bear in mind, this is only a provisional interpretation, one that we might revise from minute to minute as our encounter continues to unfold.

Dimension of Personality	Some Telltale Signs
Intelligence	Sophisticated vocabulary, correct grammar; career indications; cultural references; categorical statements; logical/linear thoughts; frequent questions
Emotionality	Tone of voice; person versus idea focus; exaggerated facial expressions; excessive sweating; fidgeting
Sociability	General chattiness; frequent eye contact; loud voice; frequent smiling/laughing; extended answers to questions; stand nearby; physical contact
Drive	One-upping/risk-taking during conversation; flashy clothes or car; loud, boisterous demeanor; conservative dress; religious jewelry and/or verbal references
Diligence	Neat or untidy dress or personal space; timeliness; references details in speech; highly organized or messy purse; prepared for various contingencies

Figure 6: Personality Cheat Sheet

REVIEW YOUR OPTIONS

IN THE BRIEF MOMENTS following an initial impression, as you form your first-glance hypothesis about the other person's leading traits, begin to process the practical implications of what you're learning. What options for action are open to you in the situation? Given your emerging quick take of the person's character, what strategies seem most promising?

In most situations, we usually have two broad options or classes of options open to us: disengaging or engaging. We can walk away and bring the encounter to an end, or we can draw closer and continue to develop it. In the fender-bender example, we could simply choose to stay in our car, keep contact with the other driver to a minimum, and wait for the police to arrive. Or we could get out and engage the driver in conversation.

Should we choose to engage, we can use the insight we gleaned from our initial read of the other person's leading trait to respond more effectively. One strategy we can deploy, familiar to good sales-people everywhere, is what psychological researchers call mirror-ing. When we notice a leading trait, our best option will usually be to mirror it in some way ourselves. By projecting familiar dimensions of personality, we can usually build rapport or ingratiate ourselves with others, subtly establishing a foundation of commonality.

If you're trying to notch a sale and your prospective customer seems like a hypercompetitive personality, give them apparent wins. Let them feel like they've beat you at something, even as you keep the bigger picture in mind. The same strategy works in reverse when someone is trying to sell something to you. I recently negoti-ated the trade-in of a car lease, and the salesman was a young, some-what aggressive, clearly competitive guy. You could tell he was an athlete (I guessed he had played college hockey or lacrosse) and he looked like had been to a keg party once or twice in his life. He was a nice guy, sociable and eager.

This salesman offered me an acceptable price on my new car, but in my view he undervalued my trade-in. After several back-and-forth offers, we found ourselves at an impasse, separated by about $1,500. Recognizing I was dealing with a hypercompetitive person, I took a different approach. I "let him win" by relenting to his trade-in offer, at the same time asking if we could reconsider the price of the new car. I offered him $1,500 less, and he ultimately agreed.

No influence strategy applies in every situation. We must fine-tune our approach to account for the personalities of the people we're seeking to influence. As you learn to practice perceptivity in the moment using the techniques described here, you won't necessarily get what you want every time, but your overall ability to influence others will increase. Best of all, those people will never see it coming.

GATHER MORE INFORMATION

IN THE INITIAL SECONDS or minutes of an encounter, after you've formed your initial quick take of personality, use the available data about a person's personality to refine your quick take and consider how best to respond. Your goal here is to slow down time, paying hyperattention to the personality factors we are facing and then deciding. When you get really good at this skill, you'll feel a little like Neo in *The Matrix*: you'll be decoding the world around you with a speed and accuracy that seems impossible. In reality, you're just catching up mentally to what your gut is already telling you. Whether you call it spidey sense, intuition, bullshit detector, or gut feel, you're already hardwired to pick up on nuances in others' behavior and infer aspects of their personality. Perceptivity harnesses and accentuates this ingrained ability of ours, bringing to it new rigor, awareness, and discipline.

To buy more time, build rapport as described earlier in this book. Engage the other person in small talk, even for just a minute or so. Doing so is usually to your advantage, not just because you can establish a friendly connection with the other person but because you can draw out new data, testing and refining your initial hypotheses. Seasoned attorneys, mediators, professional poker players, and others who must make quick decisions often make strategic use of small talk in this way. Daniel Negreanu, a professional poker player (and fellow Canadian), is a master at this. I love to watch him play on TV whenever I can. Other pro players sit at the table like the Unabomber—clad in dark sunglasses, hoodies over their head, stoic as can be. Daniel is the opposite: friendly, down-to-earth, chatty. In fact, he can't seem to shut up, a fact he willingly acknowledges. As he once remarked, "I've always been a pretty talkative guy. And that doesn't change when I come to the poker table. If you've seen me play on TV, you'll know that. I do a lot of chitchat. And one of the benefits or the side benefits I get from that is I get more information about who I'm up against, right?"[16]

Many poker players bluff, making it harder for their opponents to discern the cards that they're holding. And yet their tiniest behaviors or physical changes can serve as "tells," cues that help experienced players to predict their opponents' cards. The many books written about tells mostly advise that players look for signs of momentary changes in opponents' emotions, such as pupils dilating, pulsating neck veins, or other signs of suddenly increased heart rate. The books also advise that players look for certain behaviors, such as a player's tendency to cover their mouth. Supposedly this indicates that they have a good hand.

In truth, none of these cues have any meaning unless you also have at least some knowledge of your opponent's personality. A player who is anxious by nature will experience sudden, visible changes in heart rate that likely have nothing to do with the cards they hold. A shy player is more likely to put their hand over their mouth than their more extroverted opponents. Understanding personality gives you a reference point for judging behaviors and, with time and skill, inferring emotional state.

Of course, when playing poker we don't usually have the luxury of time to fully assess someone's personality. Our best bet is to use what information we can and get our opponents talking to elicit more data. As Negreanu reflects, "Stereotyping and profiling is obviously something we don't want to do in society, but at the poker table, every bit of information you can get about your opponent" really counts.

Profiling helps in everyday life as well, especially when we focus on gleaning information about personality. As I've noted, we must remain aware that our impressions are provisional, often rooted in stereotype, and quite possibly inaccurate. To the extent we can, we also must remain mindful of biases we harbor that might skew our judgment, and adjust our impressions accordingly. Again, what we're after in everyday situations isn't the perfect, ironclad insight that will allow us to respond successfully. We just want *some* basis for proceeding that might increase our chances of success, giving us an edge.

Once you've made small talk and have gotten down to business, consider mobilizing a variation of a tactic discussed earlier in this book: take a micro-break. A high-powered New York City attorney and client of mine recently told me that during negotiations with other attorneys she'll often prompt everyone present to step out of the conversation and take a reflective pause. "Hang on a second," she'll say. "Let's all step back and remind ourselves what our intended goals are here."

Quite often, prompting a pause will shake loose personality-related information that had previously remained hidden. The request to pause can come as a mild surprise for the other person—you'll get an unvarnished reaction of some sort. In a negotiation, pausing can allow people to take a breath and let their guard down. My client's negotiation adversary might reveal—via just a quick turn of phrase or bodily movement—something about their motivations and core character. My client might learn that the attorney on the other side of the table is a people-pleaser, looking to make a deal at any cost in order to make their client happy. She might learn that they are money-motivated and trying to delay negotiations in order to rack up hourly fees. She might learn than they are diligent by nature and that good organization and a process focus on her part will lead to the best-negotiated outcome. Taking a micro-break changes the flow of a social interaction, enabling you to deepen your personality-related insights about others.

A third tactic to keep in mind is to pay attention to how a person you're interacting with engages with others. In spontaneous situations, we often have a chance to observe brief glimpses of social interaction, whether it's how a person treats service people around them, or bickers with their significant other, or interacts with a police officer or someone else in a position of authority. These moments seem inconsequential or even bothersome—interludes during which we must patiently wait before our own encounter with someone continues. And yet such social interactions can yield valuable insight that can help us shape our own judgments.

PUTTING IT ALL TOGETHER

I'VE PRESENTED THE CHARACTER Quick Take in a stepwise way, but in many situations you should be prepared to weave fluidly back and forth through the steps. The precise order of operations doesn't matter so much here—you're just trying to mobilize your perceptivity tools as best you can to better judge others' character. When my kids were younger, I watched them do this instinctively all the time. On the soccer field, at recess, during dance class, and at sleepover camp, my children would get a quick take on people, often surprisingly accurate (but sometimes not). Then they would naturally use the tactics indicated here to sharpen their view. Indeed, children have an intuitive sense of whether someone is good or bad, friend or foe. I believe that we should nurture these natural abilities of ours just as we do other skills like our ability to analyze a problem or to consider others' points of view.

The next time you walk into a job interview with someone, try practicing the Character Quick Take. Let's say you have fifteen minutes with this stranger. Spend the first few chatting them up, asking a basic question about what they did over the weekend or what they think about the weather. Come to a quick theory of their leading trait. If they are intellectual and analytical, convey your own problem-solving abilities by describing a challenge you faced and running through the logic of how you attempted to solve it. If they seem to lead with emotionality, evoke emotion by smiling a lot and expressing how much you love the company's brand and feel passionate about its programs. If they seem to lead with sociability, spend more time chatting to come across as charming or gregarious. And so on.

Applying perspectivity in the moment is really about keeping the Personality Blueprint foremost in your mind, becoming more keenly attuned to how other people are behaving, and becoming more thoughtful and deliberate about the nuances of your own behavior. Again, this method isn't guaranteed to get you what you want. In some situations, people you encounter will have already formed impressions of you that are so strong that nothing you can do will shake them. More often, though, you have at least some room to shape how others see you. Perceptivity can give you an edge as you spontaneously engage, enabling you to steer an interaction in desirable ways. And the longer an encounter lasts, the more information you receive about the other person, and the more you can adjust and fine-tune your response.

Bear in mind, perceptivity is an in-person exercise. While you may think that you can form insights about others' personality by

Zoom (or by phone, email, or text), the truth is that you can't. Too much data is lost in translation, and you will surely make errors. The subtleties in behavior that differentiate one person from the next are simply not perceptible online. You might hope to size up a prospective mate's personality by their Hinge profile or a FaceTime "date," but that's an amateur's mistake. Put your phone down and meet the person face-to-face.

I practice Character Quick Takes all the time, sizing people up as best I can in short order and then responding in kind. When I tell people I am a psychologist, they frequently ask, "Oh, are you analyzing me right now?" Actually, I probably am. Perceptivity becomes a muscle that I immediately flex whenever I meet someone new. Beyond enhancing my skills as a psychologist and coach, it has made me a better interviewer, salesman, and, hopefully, dinner party guest.

Being able to size others up and react in the moment has been particularly helpful at make-or-break moments in my life and career. Let me share one such inflection point with you. It was 2014, and I got a call to do some work with the NBA. The league was going through a leadership succession, with the late David Stern stepping down as commissioner and his replacement, Adam Silver, taking over. Stern and Silver were thinking of hiring me to potentially support the succession and advise the two of them on leadership matters. After a few phone calls with Adam, I was invited to meet with both of them at the league's offices in Midtown Manhattan.

Although I had never met either executive before in person, I had watched David on television for years. Now I found myself waiting for him to arrive in a plush boardroom overlooking the Manhattan skyline. In walked David and Adam, and my heart skipped a beat. David struck me as incredibly charismatic, smart, and well spoken. Adam seemed equally brilliant yet somehow more diplomatic and understated. David led the conversation, and as I quickly realized, he wasn't shy about it. Most strikingly, he had a particular way of relating to others and sizing them up—he was remarkably direct in his questioning, though doing so in a charismatic and even endearing way. His style reflected a deep-seated confidence, and I suspected that he would look unfavorably on me if I didn't convey a similar confidence. I had to have guts with this guy, go toe-to-toe with him, and engage in a battle of wits.

It wasn't long before I had a chance. "Oh," he said at one point, "I see you got your PhD from York University. What the hell is York University?" Recognizing the personality I was dealing with, I reacted in kind, retorting in a way that was equally clever and showed him that I could play at his game. "You know," I said, "that's a bit like asking LeBron 'What's the deal with the Cavs?'"

This quick response marked a turning point in the conversation, the moment when I won David over. He laughed, looked at Adam, and said, "I like this guy." I got the job and began working closely with both sports business legends for the next several years. Some of my most meaningful professional experiences took place with the NBA, and I am grateful to have had this unique opportunity. It led to work with other high-profile CEOs and served as a catalyst for my firm's growth. Had I responded more tentatively to David's questioning, I am quite certain I wouldn't be where I am today.

You, too, can achieve breakthroughs like this in your life, but you have to practice perceptivity. You must pay close attention, deploying the Personality Blueprint to gain provisional insight. On the basis of this knowledge, you must thoughtfully choose behaviors that in some way mirror elements of personality that you encounter but that feel authentic to who *you* are, too. By mastering the Character Quick Take, you can forge better connections with others and get more of what you want, no matter what the situation or whom you happen to be dealing with. Crafting your behavior in this way is the art of exercising good judgment.

KEY INSIGHTS

- Character Quick Takes allow us to use insights about character in the moment to favorably influence others so that they behave as we wish.
- To perform a Character Quick Take, stay alert for initial personality cues; calibrate for context; review your options; confirm, revise, or deepen your hypothesis; and then take action.
- Character Quick Takes entail attending to verbal and nonverbal cues not as a means of understanding others' emotional states in the moment, as negotiators, poker players, and others often do, but rather their core personality traits.
- Knowing some key personality "tells" can make in-the-moment analysis easier.
- As you gain insight into personality, try to mirror what you see and use it to exercise good judgment.

CONCLUSION

Perceptivity as a Habit

WHEN I MEET SOMEONE socially for the first time and they inquire about what I do, they often ask me—jokingly, I assume—whether I'm analyzing them right now. I have some standard comebacks, and to be frank, none of them are all that clever. The truth is, I *am* analyzing them. Maybe not to the extent that they suspect or using a vocabulary that they would find familiar, but I'm definitely observing and interpreting their behavior.

At dinner, my father keeps staring at a painting on the wall in my dining room. When I ask if everything is okay, he says he can't figure out if the frame is perfectly aligned—he feels it might be off a degree or two. Alarm bells ring in my head as I recall his characteristic eye for detail. One of my friends reaches out to ask if everything is all right because I've seemed a bit distracted lately. This, I immediately realize, is evidence of his empathy and compassion. I reconnect with my old doctoral supervisor after twenty years because I see him on Twitter describing a fascinating line of research on which he's been working. We discuss possibly writing a book on it together, and I'm flooded with insights about his profound brilliance. I see my grown children Brandon, Aaron, and Lauren playing guitar or singing, and I marvel at their great creativity and expressiveness.

I've argued in this book that good judgment is a superpower any of us can cultivate, with massive implications for our careers and lives.

By deploying modern science to glean people's core personalities, we can make better people choices at work and at home, improve our performance, build and maintain stronger relationships, and exert more influence in the moment. But as I've been reminded while writing this book, good judgment isn't a tool we trot out to our advantage right when we need it. Rather, it's a skill we build, nurture, and deploy *constantly and on an ongoing basis* as we move through the world, even at moments when we're not trying to hire someone, better our relationships, and so on.

The Five Boxes, the interviewing strategies, the Partnership Road Map, the Character Quick Take—these and the other tools I've presented need to *live* with us, to the point where they become second nature. By cultivating an insatiable curiosity about people, by getting into the habit of watching them closely, and by deploying a rigorous methodology to interpret their behavior, we can become ever more adept at perceptivity and continue to deepen our insight into those around us.

Developing perceptivity as a practice and all the focus and hard work that this entails might be more than you bargained for when you picked up this book. Let me assure you, the benefits you'll accrue will be worth it. Think of all the insight you'll gain if you treat every dinner, every meeting, every hallway chat as an opportunity to gain new data about character, while also understanding your own personality and biases better.

It's not just people decisions that will improve as you make perceptivity an ingrained habit. You will, too. After all, your character is the sum total of the people decisions you've made during your life. As you make better people decisions and come to learn from your mistakes, you'll become wiser, understanding your own biases and learning to correct for them. Since you'll have a better sense of what behavior is "in character" for a given person, you'll become more

forgiving and empathetic, spotting behavior that is out of character and making allowances for it. I know that I've come a long way
since I was a child and first began playing "the Game" with my
mother on Toronto's subway. I'm a better parent, spouse, leader, and
entrepreneur—all because I've stuck with perceptivity and constantly work on enhancing my ability to read people. I'm not perfect
by any means, but I'm better.

Making perceptivity a habit also enhances your life by helping
you feel more grounded. The world around us is volatile and uncertain, especially the world of social media. What's real and what
isn't? Whom can you really trust? Practiced over time, perceptivity
gives us much more clarity. If life comes at us fast, the tools I've
presented help us to slow it down so that it becomes more deci-
pherable. We might still make mistakes, trusting or partnering
with the wrong people, but we become increasingly adept at cutting
through the noise and cueing in to the meaningful signals people
give. That clarity allows us to feel more confident and in control,
which in turn can improve our decision-making. Instead of feeling
constantly overwhelmed by fear, to the point where it informs and
constrains our choices, we can analyze our options in calmer, more
rational ways.

Perspective, empathy, clarity, maturity, self-confidence: what
we're describing here is greater *wisdom*. Most people associate wisdom with intellect, knowledge about the world, or an ability to take
a long-term perspective. But wisdom also entails greater insight
into people. We might presume that such insight comes with experience, and that's true. But we also can fast-track it by learning to
make more of every interaction we have with others.

It's tempting these days to bury ourselves in our phones and tune
others out. With the arrival of artificial intelligence, it seems even
more tempting to focus all of our attention on technology. Don't

do it. Lean even *further* into understanding the people around you. Stay curious about human behavior. Probe deeper into your own personality. As I've found, observing people and seeing how they tick isn't just a child's game, nor is it merely a tool we can use to get ahead. When you make it a habit and cultivate it over the long term, it can become a profound, empowering, and enriching way to live.

ACKNOWLEDGMENTS

THIS BOOK HAS BEEN many years in the making. Without a doubt, I learned my own good judgment from my parents, Allan and Elaine Davis. I am forever grateful for their wisdom, love, and support throughout my life. My brother, Kevin, has also been a deep source of insight and advice. One of the main values our parents instilled in us from an early age was the importance of a well-rounded education. I found my way into psychology in a most circuitous way, but it's more likely that psychology found me. There is nothing more fascinating to me than understanding why people are the way they are. I have indeed been blessed to have a meaningful career as an organizational psychologist, and I wish to thank those who taught me the professional skills that inspired the contents of this book. They include Gordon Flett, Avi Besser, Peter Stephenson, and Esther Gelcer. They also include the extraordinary psychologists and leaders at Kilberry, who truly raised my game: Katherine Alexander, Anuradha Chawla, Rebecca Slan Jerusalim, Henryk Krajewski, Aleka MacLellan, Navio Kwok, Kristen Scott, and Jacob Hammer. That team, and the bond we created throughout the life of Kilberry, means so much to me. Now we get to bring that energy to our new friends at Russell Reynolds and I am beyond excited about it.

I also acknowledge the following individuals, whom I deeply respect and who contributed to the insights I share in this book: David Hopkinson, Les Viner, Adam Silver, Adam Grant, Kerry Chandler,

Kelly Pereira, Michael Medline, Michael McCain, Jeff Rosenthal, Michael Levine, Michael Hollend, Julie Tattersall, Karen Gordon, Constantine Alexandrakis, Todd Safferstone, Ivan Bart (z-l), and my extended family: Nancy, Howie, Steve, and Sue.

This book would not have come to fruition without my incredible writing partner, Seth Schulman, who is a true professional and all-around good guy. I am also grateful to Jim Levine, Rachel Kambury, and Hollis Heimbouch for their wisdom and excellence. I feel so fortunate to have this entire team of pros at my side.

I would like to acknowledge the importance my friends have had in keeping me sane throughout the writing of this book and really for most of my life since high school. Kevin Rotenberg, Jordy Silver, Elliott Levine, Jason Berenstein, Adam Donsky, and Jeff Litman—thank you guys for always being there and for all the laughs along the way.

Finally, I wish to thank my family. While my wife, Eva, is not a psychologist, she has perhaps the best insight into others of anyone I know. Despite her better judgment, she agreed to share our lives together twenty-six years ago, and I am so incredibly grateful. Our kids, Brandon, Aaron, and Lauren, each unwittingly edited this book by listening and responding to my rants over the past few years. They are the inspiration for everything I do, at work and beyond.

NOTES

CHAPTER 1: PERSONALITY > EQ

1. "Higher Emotional Intelligence Leads to Better Decision-Making," Rotman School of Management, University of Toronto, November 19, 2013, https://www.sciencedaily.com/releases/2013/11/131119153027.htm; S. P. Chauhan and Daisy Chauhan, "Emotional Intelligence: Does It Influence Decision Making and Role Efficacy?" *Indian Journal of Industrial Relations* 43, no. 2 (October 2007): 217–38, https://www.jstor.org/stable/27768129; Randy Shattuck, "Five Reasons Professional Service Leaders Should Prize EQ Over IQ," *Forbes*, September 7, 2022, https://www.forbes.com/sites/forbescoachescouncil/2022/09/07/five-reasons-professional-service-leaders-should-prize-eq-over-iq/.

2. "The Most In-Demand Leadership and Management Skills," *Wharton Online* (blog), Wharton School, June 30, 2020, https://online.wharton.upenn.edu/blog/most-in-demand-leadership-and-management-skills/; Lauren Landry, "Why Emotional Intelligence Is Important in Leadership," *Business Insights* (blog), Harvard Business School, April 3, 2019, https://online.hbs.edu/blog/post/emotional-intelligence-in-leadership; Dori Meinert, "Emotional Intelligence Is Key to Outstanding Leadership," SHRM, February 23, 2018, https://www.shrm.org/hr-today/news/hr-magazine/0318/pages/emotional-intelligence-is-key-to-outstanding-leadership.aspx.

3. Dana Rubinstein, "The No. 1 Skill Eric Adams Is Looking For (It's Not on a Résumé)," *New York Times*, December 18, 2021, https://www.nytimes.com/2021/12/18/nyregion/eric-adams-emotional-intelligence.html.

4. Nia Prater, "Eric Adams's Approval Rating Is Falling," *New York*, February 1, 2023, https://nymag.com/intelligencer/2023/02/eric-adamss-approval-rating-is-falling.html.

5. "Did You Know That Most Emotions Last 90 Seconds? Emotions Come and Go; However, Feelings Can Last a Long Time!" Care Clinics, accessed June 26, 2023, https://care-clinics.com/did-you-know-that-most-emotions-last-90-seconds/.

6. Isobel Whitcomb, "Does Your Personality Change as You Get Older?" Live Science, August 23, 2023, https://www.livescience.com/personality-age-change.html.

7. "A Brief History of Emotional Intelligence," Socialigence, accessed June 26, 2023, https://www.socialigence.net/blog/a-brief-history-of-emotional-intelligence/.

8. Howard Gardner, *Frames of Mind: The Theory of Multiple Intelligences* (New York: Basic Books, 2011).

9. Lynn Waterhouse, "Multiple Intelligences, the Mozart Effect, and Emotional Intelligence: A Critical Review," *Educational Psychologist* 41, no. 4 (2006): 207–25, DOI:10.1207/s15326985ep4104_1.

10. Gretchen M. Whitman, "Learning Styles: Lack of Research-Based Evidence," *Clearing House: A Journal of Educational Strategies, Issues and Ideas* 96, no. 4 (2023): 111–15, DOI:10.1080/00098655.2023.2203891.

11. Peter Salovey and John D. Mayer, "Emotional Intelligence," *Imagination, Cognition, and Personality* 9, no. 3 (1989–90): 185–211.

12. Peter Salovey and John D. Mayer, "Emotional Intelligence," *Sage* 9, no. 3 (1990), https://doi.org/10.2190/DUGG-P24E-52WK-6CDG.

13. "4 Business Ideas That Changed the World: Emotional Intelligence," *HBR Ideacast* (podcast), October 27, 2022, https://hbr.org/podcast/2022/10/4-business-ideas-that-changed-the-world-emotional-intelligence.

14. Daniel Goleman, *Emotional Intelligence: Why It Can Matter More Than IQ*, 25th anniversary ed. (New York: Bantam Books, 2020), xi.

15. Goleman, 37–38.

16. Goleman, 30, 32.

17. See the front cover of *Time* magazine, October 2, 1995.

18. Daniel Goleman, "What Makes a Leader," *Harvard Business Review*, January 2004, https://hbr.org/2004/01/what-makes-a-leader.

19. Travis Bradberry, "Increasing Your Salary with Emotional Intelligence," Talent SmartEQ, accessed July 6, 2023, https://www.talentsmarteq.com/articles/increasing-your-salary-with-emotional-intelligence/. See also Lisa Evans, "Why Emotionally Intelligent People Make More Money," *Fast Company*, January 13, 2015, https://www.fastcompany.com/3040732/why-emotionally-intelligent-people-make-more-money.

20. "Jack Welch: The GE Titan Who Embodied the Flaws in Modern Capitalism," *Guardian*, March 8 2020, https://www.theguardian.com/business/2020/mar/08/jack-welch-general-electric-chairman-flaws-capitalism; "Fortune Lists Tough Bosses," UPI, July 18, 1984, https://www.upi.com/Archives/1984/07/18/Fortune-lists-tough-bosses/4419458971200/.

21. Jack Welch, "Four E's (a Jolly Good Fellow)," *Wall Street Journal*, January 23, 2004, https://www.wsj.com/articles/SB107481763013709619.

22. "Share of Organizations Conducting Training in Emotional Intelligence Worldwide in 2019, by Type," Statista, accessed June 28, 2023, https://www.statista.com/statistics/1074201/share-organizations-conducting-emotional-intelligence-training-worldwide/.

23. "Seventy-One Percent of Employers Say They Value Emotional Intelligence over IQ, According to CareerBuilder Survey," CareerBuilder, August 18, 2011, https://www.careerbuilder.ca/share/aboutus/pressreleasesdetail.aspx?id=pr652&sd=8%2f18%2f2011&ed=8%2f18%2f2099.

24. Doris Kearns Goodwin, "Lincoln and the Art of Transformative Leadership," *Harvard Business Review*, September–October 2018, https://hbr.org/2018/09/lincoln-and-the-art-of-transformative-leadership.

25. Meghna Singhal, "6 Things Emotionally Intelligent Parents Do Differently," *Psychology Today*, January 3, 2021, https://www.psychologytoday.com/us/blog/the-therapist-mommy/202101/6-things-emotionally-intelligent-parents-do

-differently; Li Wang, "Exploring the Relationship Among Teacher Emotional Intelligence, Work Engagement, Teacher Self-Efficacy, and Student Academic Achievement: A Moderated Mediation Model," *Frontiers in Psychology*, January 3, 2022, DOI:10.3389/fpsyg.2021.810559 2022.

26. Bo Hanson, "Emotional Intelligence in Sports for Elite Athletes," Athlete Assessments, June 29, 2023, https://www.athleteassessments.com/emotional-intelligence-in-sports/.

27. Alistair Gardiner, "Emotional Intelligence: Why Doctors Need to Develop This Skill," MD Linx, December 21, 2021, https://www.mdlinx.com/article/emotional-intelligence-why-doctors-need-to-develop-this-skill/dQHuxsoFAvYS0QBBPXBA0.

28. "Emotional Intelligence—Why All Police Officers Need It Civil Service Success," Civil Service Success, March 20, 2020, https://civilservicesuccess.com/emotional-intelligence-why-all-police-officers-need-it/.

29. Lisa Wintrip, "Emotional Intelligence in Today's World of Accountancy," LinkedIn, October 21, 2020, https://www.linkedin.com/pulse/emotional-intelligence-todays-world-accountancy-lisa-wintrip/; Lauren Scalzo, "Emotional Intelligence: Why You Need It, and How You Can Increase It," Stepping Stone, August 2016, https://www.soa.org/globalassets/assets/library/newsletters/stepping-stone/2016/august/stp-2016-iss63-scalzo.pdf; Wayne Duggan, "For Investors, Emotional Intelligence Is as Important as IQ," *U.S. News & World Report*, December 13, 2016, https://money.usnews.com/investing/articles/2016-12-13/for-investors-emotional-intelligence-is-as-important-as-iq.

30. Brian Koyn, "First in Emotional Intelligence: George Washington During the Newburgh Conspiracy," All Things Liberty, June 2, 2022, https://allthingsliberty.com/2022/06/first-in-emotional-intelligence-george-washington-during-the-newburgh-conspiracy/; Harvey Deutschendorf, "5 Emotional Intelligence Tips We Can Learn from One of America's Wisest Leaders," *Fast Company*, May 14, 2014, https://www.fastcompany.com/3030544/5-emotional-intelligence-tips-we-can-learn-from-one-of-americas-wisest-leaders; Adam Grant, "The Dark Side of Emotional Intelligence," *Atlantic*, January 2, 2014 https://www.theatlantic.com/health/archive/2014/01/the-dark-side-of-emotional-intelligence/282720/.

31. John D. Mayer, Peter Salovey, and David R. Caruso, "Emotional Intelligence: New Ability or Eclectic Traits?," *American Psychologist* 63, no. 6 (September 2008): 503–17.

32. Mayer, Salovey, and Caruso.

33. See, for instance, Frank J. Landy, "Some Historical and Scientific Issues Related to Research on Emotional Intelligence," *Journal of Organizational Behavior* 26, no. 4 (June 2005): 411–24; Melanie J. Schulte, M. Ree, and M. J. Schulte, "Emotional Intelligence: Not Much More than G and Personality," *Personality and Individual Differences* 37, no. 5 (October 2004): 1059–68.

34. John Antonakis, "'Emotional Intelligence': What Does It Measure and Does It Matter for Leadership?," in *Game-Changing Designs: Research-Based Organizational Change Strategies*, LMX Leadership, vol. 7, ed. G. B. Graen (Greenwich, CT: Information Age, 2010), 7.

35. John Antonakis, "Why Emotional Intelligence Does Not Predict Leadership Effectiveness: A Comment on Prati, Douglas, Ferris, Ammeter, and Buckley (2003)," *International Journal of Organizational Analysis* 11, no. 4 (2003): 355–61, https://doi.org/10.1108/eb02898.

36. Howard Schultz, "Message from Howard Schultz: Love, Responsibility Are Core to My Relationship with Starbucks," Starbucks Stories, March 16, 2022, https://stories .starbucks.com/stories/2022/message-from-howard-schultz-love-responsibility -are-core-to-my-relationship-with-starbucks/. See also Statya Nadella's *Hit Refresh: The Quest to Rediscover Microsoft's Soul and Imagine a Better Future for Everyone* (New York: Harper Busines, 2019). Bear in mind that showing emotions or being a sensitive person is only one aspect of scientifically valid EQ.

37. Sydney Finkelstein, *Superbosses: How Exceptional Leaders Master the Flow of Talent* (New York: Portfolio, 2019), 25–29. Ellison apparently mellowed as his career progressed. See David Rooke and William R. Torbert, "Seven Transformations of Leadership," *Harvard Business Review,* April 2005, https://hbr.org/2005/04/seven -transformations-of-leadership.

38. John D. Mayer, Peter Salovey, and David R. Caruso, "Emotional Intelligence: New Ability to Eclectic Traits?," *American Psychologist* 63, no. 6 (September 2008): 507.

39. Jeffrey M. Conte, "A Review and Critique of Emotional Intelligence Measures," *Journal of Organizational Behavior* 26, no. 4 (June 2005): 433–40; Chris Brandt, "University of Toronto Psychologists Suggest EQ Is Not Real," *University Herald,* November 30, 2016, https://www.universityherald.com/articles/52410/20161130/eq-emotional -quotient.htm.

40. Edwin Locke, "Why Emotional Intelligence Is an Invalid Concept," *Industrial and Organizational Behavior* 26, no. 4 (June 2005): 425–31, DOI:10.1002/job.318.

41. Marina Fiori and John Antonakis, "The Ability Model of Emotional Intelligence: Searching for Valid Measures," *Personality and Individual Differences* 50, no. 3 (February 2011): 329–34, DOI:10.1016/j.paid.2010.10.010.

42. Grant, "Dark Side of Emotional Intelligence."

43. Iskandar Aminov et al., "Decision Making in the Age of Urgency," McKinsey & Company, April 30, 2019, https://www.mckinsey.com/capabilities/people-and -organizational-performance/our-insights/decision-making-in-the-age-of -urgency.

44. CareerBuilder, "Nearly Three in Four Employers Affected by a Bad Hire, According to a Recent CareerBuilder Survey," press release, December 7, 2017, https://press .careerbuilder.com/2017-12-07-Nearly-Three-in-Four-Employers-Affected-by-a -Bad-Hire-According-to-a-Recent-CareerBuilder-Survey; Robert Half, "Half of Workers Surveyed Have Quit Due to a Bad Boss," press release, October, 8 2019, https://www.prnewswire.com/news-releases/half-of-workers-surveyed-have-quit -due-to-a-bad-boss-300933362.html.

45. Devon Delfino, "The Percentage of Businesses That Fail—and How to Boost Your Chances of Success," LendingTree, March 8, 2023, https://www.lendingtree.com /business/small/failure-rate/.

46. Marissa Levin, "The 5 Nonnegotiable Factors of Any Successful Partnership," *Inc.,* June 14, 2017, https://www.inc.com/marissa-levin/the-5-most-important-strategies -for-creating-a-successful-business-partnership.html.

47. Belinda Luscombe, "The Divorce Rate Is Dropping. That May Not Actually Be Good News," *Time,* November 26, 2018, https://time.com/5434949/divorce-rate-children -marriage-benefits/.

48. One definition of personality describes it as "an individual's characteristic patterns of thought, emotion, and behavior, together with the psychological mechanisms—

hidden or not—behind those patterns." David C. Funder, *The Personality Puzzle*, 5th ed. (New York: Norton, 2010), 5.

49. John D. Mayer, *Personal Intelligence: The Power of Personality and How It Shapes Our Lives* (New York: Scientific American/Farrar Straus & Giroux, 2014), 23.

50. Jon Geir Høyersten, "From Homer to Pinel: The Concept of Personality from Antiquity until 1800 AD," *Nordic Journal of Psychiatry* 51, no. 5 (1997), https://www.tandfonline .com/doi/abs/10.3109/08039489709090734; Mayer, *Personal Intelligence*, 4.

51. Marc-Antoine Crocq, "Milestones in the History of Personality Disorders," *Dialogues in Clinical Neuroscience* 52, no. 2 (June 2013): 147–53, https://www.ncbi.nlm.nih.gov /pmc/articles/PMC3811086/.

52. *Encyclopaedia Britannica*, s.v. "humour," June 16, 2023, https://www.britannica.com /science/humor-ancient-physiology; Matthew Smith, "Balancing Your Humors," *Psychology Today*, November 2, 2013, https://www.psychologytoday.com/us/blog/short -history-mental-health/201311/balancing-your-humors.

53. Sarah Waldorf, "Physiognomy, The Beautiful Pseudoscience," *Iris Blog*, Getty, October 8, 2012, https://blogs.getty.edu/iris/physiognomy-the-beautiful-pseudoscience/.

54. Funder, *Personality Puzzle*, 183.

55. Joshua M. Ackerman, Julie Y. Huang, and John A. Bargh, "Evolutionary Perspectives on Social Cognition," *Handbook on Social Cognition* (2012): 458–80, https://doi .org/10.4135/9781446247631.

56. Mayer, *Personal Intelligence*, 3.

57. Katherine H. Rogers and Jeremy C. Biesanz, "Reassessing the Good Judge of Personality," *Journal of Personality and Social Psychology* 117, no. 1 (2019): 197, DOI:10.1037 /pspp0000197.

58. Ethan Zell and Tara L. Lesick, "Big Five Personality Traits and Performance: A Quantitative Synthesis of 50+ Meta-Analyses," *Journal of Personality* 90, no. 4 (August 2022): 559–73, https://doi.org/10.1111/jopy.12683; Murray R. Barrick and Michael K. Mount, "The Big Five Personality Dimensions and Job Performance: A Meta-Analysis," *Personnel Psychology* 44, no. 1 (1991): 1–26, https://doi.org/10.1111/j.1744-6570.1991 .tb00688.x.

59. Neil D. Christiansen et al., "The Good Judge Revisited: Individual Differences in the Accuracy of Personality Judgments," *Human Performance* 18, no. 2 (April 2005): 140–41.

60. For example, see Rick Wartzman and Kelly Tang, "What Good Leadership Looks Like Now vs. Pre-Covid," *Wall Street Journal*, September 17, 2022, https://www.wsj.com /articles/what-good-leadership-looks-like-now-vs-pre-covid-11663180016.

61. Our ability to judge personality might also depend in some measure on whether the people we're seeking to judge are more or less readable, whether specific traits are more or less easily spotted, and whether we have enough data about people at our disposal to make judgments. Funder, *Personality Puzzle*, 198–208.

CHAPTER 2: THE PERSONALITY BLUEPRINT

1. See, for instance, Amy Gallo, "38 Smart Questions to Ask in a Job Interview," *Harvard Business Review*, May 19, 2022, https://hbr.org/2022/05/38-smart-questions-to-ask-in -a-job-interview; "Interview Questions to Ask," NFIB, accessed June 30, 2023, https: //www.nfib.com/member-vantage/employee-management/interview-questions/;

Karina Castrillo, Addison Aloian, and Jacqueline Tempera, "15 Best Questions to Ask on a First Date, According to Relationship Experts," *Women's Health*, June 23, 2023, https://www.womenshealthmag.com/relationships/a28141816/questions-to-ask-on-first-date/; Megan Sutton, Lois Shearing, and Isabelle Aron, "29 First Date Questions to Keep the Conversation Flowing," *Cosmopolitan*, updated March 21, 2023, https://www.cosmopolitan.com/uk/love-sex/relationships/a9603966/first-date-questions/; Adam Bryant, "How to Hire the Right Person," *New York Times*, accessed June 30, 2023, https://adambryantbooks.com/articles/.

2. Randy J. Larson and David M. Buss, *Personality Psychology: Domains of Knowledge about Human Nature*, 6th ed. (Dubuque, IA: McGraw-Hill Education, 2018), 63.

3. Funder, *Personality Puzzle,* 230.

4. Dan P. McAdams, "What Do We Know When We Know a Person," *Journal of Personality* 63, no. 3 (September 1995): 365–96.

5. Funder, *Personality Puzzle*, 241.

6. John M. Digman, "The Curious History of the Five Factor Model," in *The Five-Factor Model of Personality: Theoretical Perspectives*, ed. Jerry S. Wiggins (New York: Guilford Press, 1996), 1.

7. The British-American psychologist Raymond Cattell put the number at sixteen, publishing the still-used 16PF personality test. Digman, 6.

8. Digman, 5–11.

9. Gerald Goldstein and Michel Hersen, "Chapter 1—Historical Perspectives," in *Handbook of Psychological Assessment*, ed. Gerald Goldstein and Michel Hersen, 3rd ed. (London: Pergamon, 2000), 3–17, https://doi.org/10.1016/B978-008043645-6/50079-3. On the controversy surrounding the Rorschach test, see Damion Searls, "Can We Trust the Rorschach Test?," *Guardian*, February 21, 2017, https://www.theguardian.com/science/2017/feb/21/rorschach-test-inkblots-history; "What's Behind the Rorschach Inkblot Test?," BBC, July 25, 2012, https://www.bbc.com/news/magazine-18952667. See also Jerry S. Wiggins, *Paradigms of Personality Assessment* (New York: Guilford Press, 2003), 53–54.

10. Robyn M. Dawes, *House of Cards: Psychology and Psychotherapy Built on Myth* (New York: Free Press, 1994), 152–53.

11. McAdams, "What Do We Know," 372.

12. Digman, "Curious History," 13.

13. I base these descriptions of the Big Five on the American Women's College at Bay Path University's Psychology Department and Chapter 19 of Michelle McGrath, *Theories of Personality*, https://open.baypath.edu/psy321book/.

14. M. K. Mount, M. R. Barrick, and G. L. Stewart, "Five-Factor Model of Personality and Performance in Jobs Involving Interpersonal Interactions," *Human Performance* 11, no. 2–3 (1998): 145–65, https://doi.org/10.1207/s15327043hup1102&3_3.

15. M. C. Ashton, and K. Lee, "HEXACO Personality Inventory—Revised (HEXACO-PI-R)," in *Encyclopedia of Personality and Individual Differences*, ed. V. Zeigler-Hill and T. Shackelford (Cham, Switzerland: Springer, 2017), https://doi.org/10.1007/978-3-319-28099-8_900-1.

16. Boele De Raad et al., "Only Three Factors of Personality Description Are Fully Replicable Across Languages: A Comparison of 14 Trait Taxonomies," *Journal of Personality and Social Psychology* 98, no. 1 (January 2010): 160–73, DOI:10.1037/a0017184, PMID: 20053040.

17. Donald R. Lynam et al., " "Little Evidence That Honesty-Humility Lives Outside of FFM Agreeableness," *European Journal of Personality* 34, no. 4 (2020): 530–31.

18. Richard A. Davis, Gordon L. Flett, and Avi Besser, "Validation of a New Scale for Measuring Problematic Internet Use: Implications for Pre-Employment Screening," *Cyberpsychology & Behavior* 5, no. 4 (July 5, 2004): 331–45, http://doi.org/10.1089/1094 93102760275581.

19. Steven W. Rholes and Jeffry A. Simpson, "Attachment Theory: Basic Concepts and Contemporary Questions," in *Adult Attachment: Theory, Research, and Clinical Implications*, ed. W. S. Rholes and J. A. Simpson (New York: Guilford, 2004), 3–14.

20. Walter Isaacson, *Elon Musk* (Simon & Schuster, 2023).

21. Hope King, "Elon Musk Opens Up about Growing Up with Asperger's," *Axios*, April 15, 2022, https://www.axios.com/2022/04/15/elon-musk-aspergers-syndrome.

22. Aisha Counts and Tom Maloney, "Twitter Is Now Worth Just 33% of Elon Musk's Purchase Price, Fidelity Says," Bloomberg, May 30, 2023, https://www.bloomberg .com/news/articles/2023-05-30/twitter-is-worth-33-of-musk-s-purchase-price -fidelity-says.

23. "The Leadership Psychology of Linda Yaccarino: A New Hope for Twitter?" Medium, accessed July 1, 2023, https://medium.com/@receptiviti/the-leadershi-psychology -of-linda-yaccarino-a-new-hope-for-twitter-7c67db1015c3.

CHAPTER 3: THE SECRETS TO REVEALING CONVERSATIONS

1. Greg Jubb, "Under Armour Answers Questions about the SpeedForm Running Shoe," Holabird Sports, updated July 31, 2018, https://www.holabirdsports.com/blogs/news /under-armour-answers-questions-about-the-speedform-running-shoe; Under Armour, "Under Armour Doubles-Down on Connected Footwear; Unveils New Line of UA Record Equipped Running Shoes," press release, December 14, 2016, https://about.under armour.com/investor-relations/news-events-presentations/corporate-news/id/12256.

2. See, for instance, Sherry Turkle, *Reclaiming Conversation: The Power of Talk in a Digital Age* (New York: Penguin, 2015).

3. Kate Gill, "South Korea's Street Lights Up as Road Safety for Pedestrians That Stare at Their Phones While Crossing," *Independent,* accessed July 2, 2023, https://www .independent.co.uk/tv/lifestyle/south-korea-pedestrian-lights-crossing-vf6032e7b.

4. Alan Waterman, "Identity Development from Adolescence to Adulthood: An Extension of Theory and a Review of Research," *Developmental Psychology* 18, no. 3 (1982): 341–58, DOI:10.1037/0012-1649.18.3.341.

5. Dan P. McAdams, "The Psychology of Life Stories," *Review of General Psychology* 5, no. 2 (2001): 100–22, https://doi.org/10.1037/1089-2680.5.2.100.

6. Samuel D. Gosling et al., "A Room with a Cue: Personality Judgments Based on Offices and Bedrooms," *Journal of Personality and Social Psychology* 82, no. 3 (2002) 379–98. Stereotypes we might hold also affect the accuracy of our personality judgments based on the environment.

7. Mahzarin R. Banaji and Anthony G. Greenwald, *Blindspot: Hidden Biases of Good People* (New York: Delacorte Press, 2013).

8. Shai Danziger, Jonathan Levav, and Liora Avnaim-Pesso, "Extraneous Factors in Judicial Decisions," *Proceedings of the National Academy of Sciences* 108, no. 17 (2011): 6889–92, http:// dx.doi.org/10.1073/pnas.1018033108.

CHAPTER 4: THE RIGHT STUFF

1. Scientists have raised a number of objections to the Myers-Briggs exam. For instance, we expect scientific tests to be replicable. If we take them multiple times, we'll get the same result. Around half of people get a *different* result if they take Myers-Briggs again, making their results essentially meaningless. Scientists also note the paucity of evidence suggesting a relationship between results of Myers-Briggs testing and actual results in the workplace. The very conceptual underpinnings of the test are flawed. Myers-Briggs purports to tell people what personality "type" they are, based on the theories of Carl Jung. But as research has shown, personality "types" don't actually exist. People aren't "extroverts," "intuitive," "thinkers," "feelers," or some combination of such types, as proponents of the Myers-Briggs test would have us believe. Rather, people possess traits across a spectrum, manifesting them differently and to different degrees depending on the context. See Adam Grant, "Say Goodbye to MBTI, the Fad That Won't Die," LinkedIn, September 17, 2013, https://www.linkedin.com/pulse/20130917155206-69244073-say-goodbye-to-mbti-the-fad-that-won-t-die/; Joseph Stromberg and Estelle Caswell, "Why the Myers-Briggs Test Is Totally Meaningless," *Vox*, updated October 8, 2015, https://www.vox.com/2014/7/15/5881947/myers-briggs-personality-test-meaningless.

2. John Tierney, "A Match Made in the Code," *New York Times*, February 11, 2013, https://www.nytimes.com/2013/02/12/science/skepticism-as-eharmony-defends-its-matchmaking-algorithm.html; "ASA Ruling on eHarmony UK Ltd," Advertising Standards Authority, January 3, 2018, https://www.asa.org.uk/rulings/eharmony-uk-ltd-a17-392456.html.

3. Ruchika Tulshyan, "Don't Hire for Culture Fit," Society for Human Resource Management Executive Network, March 15, 2022, https://www.shrm.org/executive/resources/articles/pages/dont-hire-for-culture-fit-tulshyan.aspx.

4. Deniz S. Ones et al., "In Support of Personality Assessment in Organizational Settings," *Personnel Psychology* 60, no. 4 (2007): 995–1027, https://doi.org/10.1111/j.1744-6570.2007.00099.x.

5. "When Hiring Execs, Context Matters Most," *Harvard Business Review*, September–October 2017, https://hbr.org/2017/09/when-hiring-execs-context-matters-most.

6. Kurt Eichenwald, "Microsoft's Lost Decade," *Vanity Fair*, July 24, 2012, https://www.vanityfair.com/news/business/2012/08/microsoft-lost-mojo-steve-ballmer.

CHAPTER 5: SETTING RELATIONSHIPS UP FOR SUCCESS

1. Alfred F. Tallia et al., "Seven Characteristics of Successful Work Relationships," *Family Practice Management* 13, no. 1 (2006): 47–50, https://www.aafp.org/pubs/fpm/issues/2006/0100/p47.html; Emma Seppälä and Nicole K. McNichols, "The Power of Healthy Relationships at Work," *Harvard Business Review*, June 21 2022, https://hbr.org/2022/06/the-power-of-healthy-relationships-at-work; "How to Build Good Working Relationships at Work," Indeed, updated March 10, 2023, https://www.indeed.com/career-advice/starting-new-job/how-to-build-good-working-relationships.

2. See, for instance, Mark Byford, Michael D. Watkins, and Lena Triantogiannis, "Onboarding Isn't Enough," *Harard Business Review*, May–June 2017, https://hbr.org/2017/05/onboarding-isnt-enough.

CHAPTER 6: IMPROVING PERFORMANCE

1. "Discover Who You Are—and Own It," Gallup, accessed July 4, 2023, https://www
.gallup.com/cliftonstrengths/en/253850/cliftonstrengths-for-individuals.aspx. See
also Marcus Buckingham and Donald O. Clifton, *Now, Discover Your Strengths: The
Revolutionary Gallup Program That Shows You How to Develop Your Unique Talents
and Strengths,* 20th ed. (New York: Gallup, 2020).

2. This paragraph combines text from Hogan's website and copy that appeared on an
actual Hogan test report from 2013. See "Hogan Development Survey," Hogan Assessments, accessed July 5, 2023, https://www.hoganassessments.com/assessment
/hogan-development-survey/. See also "Subscale Interpretive Guide," Hogan Assessments, October 2, 2014, 2, http://www.hoganassessments.com/sites/default/files
/uploads/HDS_Subscale_Interp_Guide_10.2.14.pdf; "11 Ways to Wreck Your Career," Hogan Assessments, January 11, 2015, https://www.hoganassessments.com
/wp-content/uploads/2015/01/11_Ways_HDS_eBook.pdf.

3. "Goodbye ACC, Hello Scotiabank Arena! Home of Leafs, Raptors Has New Name," CBS
News, updated July 3, 2018, https://www.cbc.ca/news/canada/toronto/air-canada
-centre-renamed-scotiabank-arena-1.4732410.

CHAPTER 7: INFLUENCING OTHERS

1. F. J. Lanceley, "Antisocial Personality as a Hostage-Taker," *Journal of Police Science
and Administration* 9, no. 1 (March 1981): 28–34, https://www.ojp.gov/ncjrs/virtual
-library/abstracts/antisocial-personality-hostage-taker. See also T. Strentz, "Inadequate Personality as a Hostage Taker," *Journal of Police Science and Administration* 11, no. 3 (September 1983): 363–68, https://www.ojp.gov/ncjrs/virtual-library
/abstracts/inadequate-personality-hostage-taker.

2. Lanceley, "Antisocial Personality as a Hostage-Taker." See also Strentz, "Inadequate
Personality as a Hostage Taker."

3. "What Makes a Tyrant Tick? Ask a Political Psychologist," *Yale Medicine Magazine,*
Fall/Winter 2004, https://medicine.yale.edu/news/yale-medicine-magazine/article
/what-makes-a-tyrant-tick-ask-a-political/.

4. Thorsten Hofmann, "Distant Profiling—Knowing How Your Opponent Works," C4
Institute, Quadriga University Berlin, January 16, 2019, https://negotiation-blog.eu
/distant-profiling-knowing-how-your-opponent-works/.

5. "What Makes a Tyrant Tick?"

6. *The Bourne Identity,* directed by Doug Liman, Universal Studios Home Entertain-
ment, 2008, 1:59.

7. Giovanni Angioni, "Common Poker Tells—How to Read People in Poker," Poker
News, December 4, 2019, https://www.pokernews.com/strategy/10-hold-em-tips-5
-common-poker-tells-to-look-for-25433.htm.

8. Neil H. Katz and Adriana Sosa, "The Emotional Advantage: The Added Value of the
Emotionally Intelligent Negotiator," *Conflict Resolution Quarterly* 33, no. 1 (Fall 2015):
57–74, https://doi.org/10.1002/crq.21127; Tomas Chamorro-Premuzic, "The Personality Traits of Good Negotiators," *Harvard Business Review,* August 7, 2017, https://
hbr.org/2017/08/the-personality-traits-of-good-negotiators.

9. Alison Wood Brooks, "Emotion and the Art of Negotiation," *Harvard Business Review,*
December 2015, https://hbr.org/2015/12/emotion-and-the-art-of-negotiation.

10. Hillary Anger Elfenbein et al., "Reading Your Counterpart: The Benefit of Emotion Recognition Accuracy for Effectiveness in Negotiation," *Journal of Nonverbal Behavior* 31 (2007): 205–23, https://doi.org/10.1007/s10919-007-0033-7.

11. Paul Ekman, "Facial Expressions," in *The Science of Facial Expression, Social Cognition, and Social Neuroscience,* ed. James A. Russell and José-Miguel Fernández-Dols (New York: Oxford University Press, 2017), 39–56, https://doi.org/10.1093/acprof:oso/9780190613501.003.0003.

12. Adam Grant, *Think Again: The Power of Knowing What You Don't Know* (New York: Viking, 2021).

13. For research suggesting the accuracy of first impressions, see Laura P. Naumann et al., "Personality Judgments Based on Physical Appearance," *Personal and Social Psychology Bulletin* 35, no. 12 (December 2009): 1661–71, https://doi.org/10.1177/0146167209346309. For research suggesting inaccuracy or variation in first impressions, see Alexander Todorov and Jenny M. Porter, "Misleading First Impressions: Different for Different Facial Images of the Same Person," *Psychological Science* 25, no. 7 (July 2014): 1404–17, DOI:10.1177/0956797614532474, e-pub May 27, 2014. We often are unable to distinguish whether our personality judgments are accurate or not: Daniel R. Ames et al., "Not So Fast: The (Not-Quite-Complete) Dissociation Between Accuracy and Confidence in Thin-Slice Impressions," *Personality and Social Psychology Bulletin* 36, no. 2 (February 2010): 264–77, https://doi.org/10.1177/0146167209354519.

14. Charles C. Ballew II and Alexander Todorov, "Predicting Political Elections from Rapid and Unreflective Face Judgments," *Proceedings of the National Academy of Sciences* 104, no. 46 (2007): 17948–53, https://doi.org/10.1073/pnas.0705435104.

15. Francesca Gino, "To Negotiate Effectively, First Shake Hands," *Harvard Business Review,* June 4, 2014, https://hbr.org/2014/06/to-negotiate-effectively-first-shake-hands.

16. Daniel Negreanu, "Table Talk," Masterclass, accessed July 6, 2023, https://www.masterclass.com/classes/daniel-negreanu-teaches-poker/chapters/table-talk.

ABOUT THE AUTHOR

RICHARD DAVIS, PHD, is an organizational psychologist and managing director at Russell Reynolds Associates, a global leadership advisory firm. He has extensive experience advising CEOs, including those leading Fortune 100 companies or otherwise in the public eye. His clients include Under Armour, Target, Endeavor, the National Basketball Association, Canada Goose, L Catterton, Best Buy, and RBC. He has also assessed senior executives and board members from companies such as Microsoft, Apple, Nike, Starbucks, Amazon, General Motors, Walmart, Home Depot, UnitedHealthcare, and Google. He is the author of *The Intangibles of Leadership* and has appeared on national television and in print media, including the *Wall Street Journal*, CNN Money, *BusinessWeek*, the *Globe and Mail*, CNBC, and *Harvard Business Review*.